THE

Network

TO

Home Repair
AND **Decorating**
Services

by Ellen Laird and Barbara Brunhouse

LAIRHOUSE

Service providers are listed in "The Network to Home Repair and Decorating" based on recommendations of satisfied customer. The authors accept no liability for loss, damage or inconvenience experienced by consumers as a result of utilization of any of the Service Providers listed herein.

We would like to thank all those who helped us create this book by completing a survey and providing quotes. Your patience and good humor throughout our project was truly appreciated. We couldn't have done it without you!

Published by
Lairhouse

ISBN: 0-9660791-0-8

CONTENTS

INTRODUCTION

For years we dealt with the difficulties of finding the right person or business to handle different jobs that needed to be done to our homes. It was often frustrating to spend time tracking down contractors, painters, plumbers, upholsterers, window washers...and more.

There is an overwhelming amount of guides available to the consumer in areas such as restaurant and travel, but there really are no guides that provide information about businesses and tradespeople who do work in the home. It is for this reason that we decided to compile our own guide and simplify the process for other home owners, condo owners and apartment residents.

From the inception, we felt that all recommendations should come from satisfied customers and that the way to accomplish this was through "networking." We gathered friends, relatives and friends of friends and so on to form a large network of consumers within the designated geographical area of Somerset, Middlesex, Morris, Union and Warren counties.

Each consumer was asked to complete a survey form and the initial criteria was that each business needed at least two positive recommendations to be included in the book. The recommended businesses that wanted to be in the book provided background information from which the descriptions were written. As an added personal touch, the consumers who gave the original endorsements were then asked for quotes.

Interestingly, the #1 complaint from the consumer "network" was that too many businesses were non-responsive. So we decided to make that another criteria. After telephoning three times and receiving no reply to our calls, we eliminated that business. Some businesses returned the call and expressed an interest in being included, but subsequently did not send the required information on time...or at all. These names are listed at the back of the book and are categorized by trade.

The Network to Home Repair and Decorating Services leads the user to a list of professionals who were recommended for their excellent work and service. They are not rated, and the difference in size of each description is related only to the amount of information provided. Please note that while every effort has been made to include only top quality businesses, this guide cannot personally guarantee work that is done.

Over a year was spent developing our "network" guide and we sincerely hope it will help you complete all your home projects with ease.

—Barbara and Ellen

EXPLANATION OF CODES

The following codes appear after the telephone number of each business. They indicate which of the five counties are the preferable service areas:

MIC – Middlesex County
MC – Morris County
SC – Somerset County
UC – Union County
WC – Warren County
A – All counties

All information including telephone numbers, county codes, business name, etc., were furnished by the businesses. Telephone numbers were checked and re-checked by the authors and as of printing were correct.

AIR CONDITIONING & HEATING

A. Abcal Heating & Cooling Inc., (800)273-7793, UC MC SC, 27 years in business
Abcal installs systems as if they were going into their own homes. They fabricate their own sheet metal in-house. If the customer's HVAC system does not work properly, "they might as well be living in a cave." Therefore customer comfort and reliability is very important to this firm.

- *"They did an excellent job installing our AC/heating system. We found them to be honest and dependable. Whenever you need them, they're there. I can highly recommend them."*

Air Design Heating & Cooling Inc., (908)789-0999, UC SC MIC, 17 years in business
This is a family-owned-and-operated business. They specialize in servicing all brands of heating and cooling systems, humidification, air cleaning and sheet metal. They will install several major brands of heating and cooling systems and strive to provide prompt, personalized and dependable service.

- *"We use him for our air conditioner and heater. We like him for he is always willing to come out whenever he is needed. If he is away on vacation and we call, he will return calls immediately."*
- *"He is very dependable and comes out on a regular basis to service our units."*

Baran's Heating & Air Conditioning, (732)382-7833, LL, 30 years in business
Marty Baran provides reliable sales, service and installation of heating and AC systems. He actively looks for the most efficient way to resolve his customer's environmental problems.

- *". . . extremely reliable. Always tells the most efficient way to satisfy a problem and comes whenever I need him."*
- *"I never have any problems with any of the work he has done. He's not intrusive—wipes his feet and even takes his shoes off if muddy."*

Bernie's Heating & Cooling, (908)486-5542, A, 20 years in business
Bernard Zofcin considers every job a custom job. He will install heating and air conditioning and repair and service these systems. Sheet-metal fabrication is another specialty of his.

- *"I work for the gas company and see the work he does. When we do an inspection, I have come to know his work. On his new installation jobs and every job his work is done to perfection and he does not cut any corners. He is extremely neat*

1

and meticulous. All the customers tell me when I do the inspection that they were very pleased with his work."

- *"He is very knowledgeable and prompt. The quality of work is to perfection and customers always have good things to say about Bernie."*

C & D Cooling & Heating Co. Inc., (908)647-1696, UC MC SC, 28 years in business

Built almost exclusively from customer recommendations, this company prides itself on installing air conditioning in homes thought impossible to air condition. They attempt to match expertise and know-how to the customer's problems and needs.

- *"They installed a new heating and air contitioning system in a renovation project we were doing four years ago. When we needed service to get some of the kinks out of the unit, they responded very quickly and did a wonderful job."*
- *"I remember that they once came on a Sunday and we really appreciated that. We will continue to use them because they are prompt and responsive. We are very pleased."*

C.E.T. Heating & Air Conditioning, Inc., (908)665-2180, UC MC SC, 15 years in business

Providing service and installation of heating and air conditioning equipment for commercial and residential areas, this company is proud of their personalized service. In addition they do sheet-metal work.

- *"I love this guy. When we moved into our home he was just starting out. Our inspection report on the furnace was not good. He came, knew what he was doing and installed a new furnace."*
- *"He took into consideration the type of home we had and our needs. He installed an AC system also and in seven years we have had no problems with either unit."*

Chapman Bros., (908)276-1320, UC, 65 years in business

Founded in 1932 by Walter and Chester Chapman this business has been family-run since inception and presently employs nine people. They install, service, and repair boilers, furnaces, central air-conditioning systems, water heaters, humidifiers, air cleaners and do remodeling of old systems.

- *"Responsive and competent."*

Cool-O-Matic Inc., (908)722-6566, A, 30 years in business

From large custom-built homes to small condos, no job is too difficult for this firm. An added benefit is their ability to install home automation systems.

- *"They installed our AC system. We have had no problems and I would highly recommend them."*

_____
_____
_____

Dyna-Temp Inc., (908)687-3304, UC MC SC MIC, 17 years in business
All types of heating and AC systems are installed and serviced by Dyna-Temp; including hot air furnaces, hot water boilers, steam boilers, central air-conditioning and air purification systems. Sheet metal is measured and fabricated in-house.
- *"They installed an AC and heat system in a new three-room addition to our home three years ago. We have never had a problem."*
- *". . . air conditioned our home which is old and was a very difficult job. The three men that did the installation were absolutely superior workers and very considerate of my needs. They were exceptionally neat and clean. This was a job that I totally dreaded and they made it pain-free."*

_____
_____
_____

Ferguson Air Conditioning, Inc., (908)356-5333, A, 18 years in business
Ferguson works with residential and light commercial properties. Being a small firm, they provide quality installation of heating /AC systems, sheet-metal ducts, humidifiers and air cleaners.
- *"They did a very nice job installing our CAC system. Best of all was his accessability. He phoned when he was supposed to."*
- *". . . nice, neat work on our ducts and they didn't ruin any part of the basement."*

_____
_____
_____

Fras-Air Contracting, (800)339-1153, UC SC, 24 years in business
All of Fras-Air's employees receive extensive training not only in servicing equipment but also in providing a pleasant experience for the customer. Employees wear uniforms and are trained to explain to customers what they are doing. Follow-up is timely. Customer records are maintained so that service calls are expedited efficiently. All types of heating, air-conditioning and ventilation systems are provided.
- *"Dependable, polite, courteous people. I have used them for seven years and they actually take their shoes off and walked around on my Oriental carpets."*
- *"I never had any problems with them or the quality of their work."*

_____
_____
_____

Globe Fuel Company, (908)245-0333, UC, 50 years in business
Globe Fuel serves the needs of its customers because it understands the needs of its neigh-

bors. This is a community-based business that prides itself by standing by its principles and being accountable to customers. They started out selling coal and eventually converted to the sale of home heating oil.

- *"I like doing business with a company that has been family-run for generations. They are very customer-oriented and provide excellent service and maintenance."*

Griffing Heating & Air Conditioning Inc., (908)789-2256, UC SC MIC, 30 years in business
Providing prompt, competent service and first-class installation is a goal of Griffing. They also have an emergency repair service available.

- *"Through two installations of heating systems over a 10-year period, including recently two heating zones and full air conditioning, this company has proven to be professional. knowledgeable and competent."*
- *"Mr. Griffing takes special pains with courtesy and interest to explain the best options and keep the customer informed."*

Ketzenberg & Org Inc., (732)634-8000, A, 50 years in business
This company has a reputation for quality workmanship and prompt service. Heating and AC service has extended to thousands of satisfied customers whether it be residential or light commercial properties.

- *"They are highly reliable. They always come the same day as called."*

Koegel Plumbing & Heating Inc., (908)236-7550, A, 35 years in business
Custom designed heating systems whether it be hydronic, hot water, steam or radiant are this firm's specialty. They also provide a troubleshooting and diagnostic service for all systems including those that were improperly installed.

- *"Wonderfully reliable and extremely knowledgeable about my arcane heating system."*

Benedict Maulbeck Heating & Electrical Co., (908)277-3555, UC MC, 43 years in business
"Pete" Maulbeck prefers working on mostly residential properties. Clean and crisp are adjectives they use for describing the quality of work they provide. Whether it be heating, air conditioning, electrical design, or installation of steam, hot water and forced air-heating systems, they strive for perfection.

- *"He installed our gas heating system—very knowledgeable."*

- *"He invented a radiant heat system, a process by which he installed pipes underneath a sunporch floor. We would recommend him very highly."*

McDowells Plumbing, Heating & Air Conditioning, (908)233-8139, A, 70 years in business
This full-service company has a complete installation department for plumbing, heating and AC systems along with a component sales staff to insure the system is right for each customer.

- *". . . extremely knowledgeable and helpful. Prompt, efficient and reliable."*
- *"We have a very expensive, fancy heating system installed by the previous owners. The parts are hard to find and hard to get but McDowells repairs the system with no problems. They are always honest about how long it will take to get the parts."*

Meyer & Depew Co., (908)272-2100, A, 42 years in business
Meyer & Depew install heating and AC systems. They are a well-known community-based company whose trucks can be seen in all five counties serviced.

- *"They are prompt, reliable and do very satisfactory work. They have polite employees."*
- *"A good reputable company. Installed our heating system and do annual maintenance. Excellent service!"*

New Jersey Mechanical Contractors, (908)494-1914, A, 6 years in business
Heating, air conditioning, ventilation, sheet metal and piping can all be custom installed by New Jersey Mechanical Contractors. Their service, as they would say is prompt, keeping the customers #1.

- *"They have done so many things for me it is hard to list them all. They installed my AC unit in a very professional manner and I have used them for other electrical work. They are great!"*

Ortalis Corporation, (908)753-8100, UC MC SC MIC, 59 years in business
When everything runs but the system doesn't perform this company digs in to diagnose the problem and find the solution. They supply heating and AC service installation and design for commercial and residential properties.

- *"Installed our AC system. Their service is excellent, very responsive, always on time and very helpful."*

AIR CONDITIONING & HEATING

Petro, (908)396-8824, A, 94 years in business

All technicians working for Petro are state-certified. They provide service 24 hours a day, 365 days a year and use no subcontractors. Their C.A.R.E. (Clean-up for Accidental Release to the Environment) program is exclusive to their customers.

- *"We have been using them since we moved into our home several years ago. They installed a furnace. They deliver oil on schedule and come regularly. They have provided a very good service."*

Reel-Strong Fuel Company, (888)480-0901, UC, 72 years in business

Reel-Strong has a motto: "Big enough to serve, yet small enough to care." Being a small, family-run business, their customers can always feel confident, for an owner is always available to help solve a problem.

- *". . . installed heating and AC system. Very efficient and had excellent follow-up service."*
- *"I have used them for years. They installed our air filtering system and we have had no problems. I also happen to really like the people who run the company."*

Ryan Heating Cooling, (908)687-4300, A, 60 years in business

Ryan specializes in the installation and service of heating, ventilation and AC systems. They employ 20 people including a field staff of 14 and have 14 vehicles on the road. They feel that the most important part of their service is the selection of the technical staff. They have invested tremendously in staff schooling, seminars and conduct a daily debriefing where they discuss the previous day's issues.

- *"They installed a heating and AC system. Wonderfully friendly and helpful employees."*
- *"I was impressed with a particular computer program they have which after you put certain information into it (for example: exterior make-up of the house, window type, size of home, direction house faces), it will then tell you the proper size unit to install and the size ducts to run. This is so the unit installed does not overwhelm the house."*

SR Heating & Cooling, (973)635-2020, UC MC SC, 50 years in business

SR has been designing and installing heating and AC systems for half a century. They pride themselves on providing quality installations to residential customers.

- *". . . installed our AC system and (knock wood) we've had no problems. They're really nice people!"*

Thermal Design Engineering Inc., (908)561-1155, UC SC MIC, 11 years in business
Forced-air heating systems are the main area of concentration for this firm. Offering a 24-hour service on their installations of heating, air conditioning and sheet-metal duct-work fabrication is a plus for their customers.
- *"They have installed four furnaces and four air conditioners in my home. They are a pleasure to work with and very prompt when responding to a call."*

Volpe Service Company Inc., (973)740-1606, UC MC, 35 years in business
Commercial and residential HVAC systems are installed and serviced by this company.
- *". . . very reliable. They installed an air-conditioning system in my place of work. They provided excellent service and never a problem."*

Westfield Refrigeration & Air Conditioning Co., (908)232-5070, UC SC WC, 29 years in business
Westfield Refrigeration provides residential and commercial air conditioning, gas heating and commercial refrigeration service. They are a local established business with a quick, dependable, professional staff.
- *"Air conditioning our business was something we thought couldn't be done because it was a difficult job. They figured out how to do it. Did a great job!"*
- *"He installed AC in my home. He's very responsive and knows what he's doing. He also installed a motor in my wine cellar and maintains it."*

APPLIANCE REPAIR

APPLIANCE REPAIR

Aaron's Refrigeration, (800)962-9979, UC MC SC MIC, 30 years in business

Aaron's specializes in repair and sales of Sub-Zero refrigerators, freezers and ice makers.

- *"This is my Sub-Zero guy. If you have a Sub-Zero this is the person to call. I think there is nothing worse than a refrigerator that is not working—or there is water leaking all over the floor. It's a catastrophe. Well, Aaron's gets back to you in a second."*

American Pride Appliance Inc., (908)889-8348, UC SC MIC, 11 years in business

This is an independent authorized servicer for the majority of appliance manufacturers. This distinction allows them to service products which are newly purchased and still under warranty as well as the appliances which their customers have owned for many years. They take pride in being entrusted by so many fine companies with the care of their products. They are factory-authorized to repair the following: Whirlpool, KitchenAid, Roper, Estate, Amana, Speed Queen, Caloric, Frigidaire, White Westinghouse, Tappan, O'Keefe & Merrit, WC Woods, Gibson, Maytag, Magic Chef, Admiral, Norge, Creda, Regency, Peerless, Premier and DCS.

- *"We have used them many times for all kinds of appliance repair. They are extremely reliable, always prompt and honest. They are helpful in taking care of the little things over the phone. I have no hesitation recommending them."*

Appliance Doctor Inc., (908)232-3331, UC MIC, 11 years in business

Steven Josefovitz, the Appliance Doctor, will make house calls on all brands of major appliances.

- *"He fixed my dishwasher. Very prompt response to my phone calls. Came the same day. He was very pleasant and I would definitely use him again."*

Appliance Guy, (732)560-1970, UC SC MIC, 4 years in business,

All major appliances—all makes and models—are serviced by the Appliance Guy. They will also repair air-conditioning systems

- *"Prompt response. He has flexible hours for working people."*
- *"He does quality repairs and we have never had any problems after he repaired any of my appliances."*

Desnoyers Appliance & Television Inc., (908)756-2997, UC MC SC MIC, 78 years in business

This is one of the oldest appliance businesses in New Jersey. The sales staff is professional and they strive to guide their customers to come to the right decision concerning appliances. They not only service what they sell but will also repair existing appliances that are causing problems. Their motto is, "We treat the customer the way we would want to be treated."

- *"We have bought all our appliances from them. Their repair service is excellent. Over the years I felt that we really have had a nice relationship with them."*
- *"They have serviced appliances in my home for many years. They are very accommodating and the service is excellent. They're a nice local business that has been established for many years."*

✍ _____

_____

_____

George's Appliance Co., (908)665-1717, UC MC SC MIC, 30 years in business

Along with repairing washers, dryers, refrigerators, dishwashers, ranges and microwaves, this company is factory-authorized to repair Whirlpool, KitchenAid, Roper, Bosch, Peerless Premier, U Line and Marvel.

- *"They are very prompt and professional. I am pleased that they were extremely neat and tidy."*
- *"They installed a dishwasher and garbage disposal, repaired a microwave oven. I can recommend them very highly."*
- *"They came quickly and took care of numerous appliance problems."*

✍ _____

_____

_____

Jeff's Appliance Repair Service, (908)232-4906, UC, 21 years in business

This former employee of Austers in Westfield repairs washers, dryers, dishwashers, refrigerators, ovens, AC units, disposals and dehumidifiers. He is an active member of the Refrigeration Society and is EPA certified.

- *"Picked up where Austers left off. He is reliable and has quick service."*
- *"He worked on my washing machine. My mother, aunt and neighbor also use him and are quite satisfied."*
- *"He's a doll. A great guy. So prompt and you never have to wait. He repaired my stove, dryer and refrigerator."*

✍ _____

_____

_____

Pelzar Services Inc., (973)473-4200, A, 15 years in business

Pelzar specializes in high-end and specialty domestic kitchen, bar and family room products. They will service manufacturers warranties for: ASko, Scotsman Refrigeration, U Line refrigeration products and Viking ranges.

- *"We had a new kitchen put in one year ago. On and off there were problems with the dishwasher. Finally we had Pelzar check it out and it turned out the plumber had installed it incorrectly. He was the first guy to realize what the actual problem was and I will use him for all my appliance repairs."*

- *"He responds immediately to my phone calls. He is quick, neat and a really nice guy."*

✍ _____

_____

_____

The Repair Shack, (908)464-0797, A, 23 years in business

The Repair Shack specializes in small appliance and electronics repair. They will work on audio/video equipment, TV, VCR, stereo, vacuums, sewing machines, electric shavers, microwaves and more. They have a free pick-up and delivery service and are an authorized service for many companies.

- *"Very personable and pleasant people to deal with. They will tell you if something does not need to be fixed or is not worth it. Very honest. If an appliance needs parts they are usually able to get it."*

✍ _____

_____

_____

Spinello Appliance Service, (908)753-5520, UC MC SC, 26 years in business

Paul Spinello has a small family business that repairs and services all brands of refrigerators, washers, dryers, dishwashers, freezers, stoves and ovens. He guarantees customer satisfaction.

- *"This man is a godsend—a real find. He's very responsive and calls within 24 hours and usually comes within 24 hours. He knows how to fix any appliance—large or small. He's neat, clean, a nice guy and definitely pleasant to have around. What more can I say?"*
- *"He's very honest and forthright. Extremely responsive—always comes whenever you call him. He always gives us a good assessment of the problem. If he thought a repair was too expensive he would tell us that it wasn't worth doing."*

✍ _____

_____

_____

APPRAISERS

Dawsons Auctioneers & Appraisers, (973)984-6900, A, 20 years in business
Dawsons provides a personalized service to their customers. They do expert consultations and appraisal of fine and decorative art, antiques, furniture, silver and jewelry.
- *"When I have had work done by Dawsons, I have felt very comfortable with their knowledge and—most of all—their integrity. They are extremely professional yet approachable. You feel you can talk to them without being talked down to."*

Harry Ekizian, (212)683-1055, A, 35 years in business
Harry Ekizian appraises Oriental rugs—either antique or semi-antique. He will provide consulting and has a search service for rare and special weavings.
- *"Honesty is his trademark. He's a great guy—very sincere."*
- *"This is a family business around for two generations. They are very well-qualified appraisers."*

Abigail Hartmann Associates, (212)316-5406, A, 12 years in business
Abigail Hartmann Associates is a fine- and decorative-arts appraisal and consulting firm. Staff members belong to the American Society of Appraisers and the Appraisers Association of America. Their computerized appraisals are carefully researched and documented and accurately reflect current market trends. The experienced in-house staff is assisted by a network of experts in museums, galleries and universities. They will appraise fine art, antiques, jewelry, silver, porcelain, pottery, objets d'art, and other residential and commercial contents. Appraisals are done for the purposes of estate, gift tax, charitable contribution, insurance, damage/loss equitable distribution and resale.
- *"This firm has established a wonderful reputation for providing professionally written and researched appraisals. The staff is extremely knowledgeable and easy to work with. You can be guaranteed that the appraisal will be done well and will stand up to any scrutiny."*

Heffernan, Leger & Associates, (908)236-7098, A, 25 years in business
These appraisers have extensive experience in all phases of real property valuation. They are state-certified and designated members of the Appraisal Institute. All their reports conform with the Uniform Standards of Professional Appraisal Practice (USPAP). They understand the intricacies of real property valuation and employ applicable approaches to value.

11

- *"They have a fine reputation and a great deal of expertise. I always recommend them."*

✍ _____
_____
_____
_____

Betty Ann Morgan & Associates, (908)722-8429, A, 20 years in business
Betty is a certified appraiser of clocks, antiques and decorative arts. She will determine replacement cost for insurance purposes, fair market value of personal property for sale, estate tax, donation, dissolution of marriage and equitable distribution. She will assist and consult with clients in locating the "right" source to liquidate or find the correct way to proceed.
- *"She appraised watches and clocks in my parents' home. She was professional in every way. A wonderful person . . . extremely knowledgeable in her profession."*
- *"She has done many appraisals for me and my family. She's very efficient and takes her profession very seriously. I think that is what makes her so good at what she does."*

✍ _____
_____
_____
_____

Milton L. Ogintz Inc., (800)8-GEMS4U, A, 42 years in business
Milton Ogintz is an appraiser of diamonds and estate jewelry. He will supply the client with completely researched, computer-generated appraisals for insurance, purchase valuation, estates and equitable distribution purposes. All appraisals are done by certified gemologists.
- *"I used him to appraise some jewelry. He is a very reputable appraiser and he came highly recommended. A real nice guy."*

✍ _____
_____
_____

P.T.K. Oriental Rug Center, (973)376-0730, A, 22 years in business
Oriental rugs, new and old, can be appraised by P.T.K. They pride themselves on their knowledge and a good reputation that comes with over 22 years of experience.
- *"Our relationship goes back a number of years. They are very professional and honest. You can rely on their judgment. They are quite knowledgeable from my perspective."*
- *"They have a good eye for quality rugs and they know the market very well. A good eye for design, color and size."*

✍ _____
_____
_____

APPRAISERS

12

Swain Galleries, (908)756-1707, A, 129 years in business

Swain has a staff of appraisers specializing in 19th- and 20th-century paintings, water-colors, etchings, engravings and lithographs. Appraisals are written for insurance, estate, equitable distribution and donation purposes. All appraisals are researched and comput-er-generated and conform to the guidelines set up by USPAP.

- *"It's so important to have valuable objects appraised by someone reputable. I never worried about Swain's honesty . They were very thorough and went over all my objects with care. The appraisal was well-written and "right on the money."*

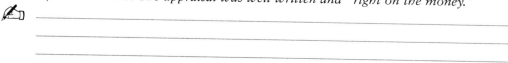

Jane H. Willis Appraisal Service, (201)569-6669, A, 19 years in business

This personal property appraiser will write appraisals for antique American furniture, decorative arts, silver and residential furnishings. She has the fortuitous combination of academic expertise, professional knowledge and extensive experience combined with real personal skills.

- *"Jane Willis has the patient, quiet nature that is so appealing in an appraiser. Upon meeting her, you know that she will do a very thorough job and in the end, the client will have an appraisal that would please even the IRS."*

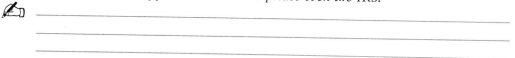

APPRAISERS

ARCHITECTS

Architecture Plus, (908)707-8100, A, 7 years in business

This firm is dedicated to providing a quality, building-design service. They utilize the latest technology in Computer Aided Drafting and Design (CADD) which provides clear, accurate, well-coordinated documents. Revisions and changes are made quickly and easily. They coordinate with the necessary consultants and agencies, educate clients of possible design solutions, guide them through the decision-making process and strive to provide a final product that fulfills the client's needs.

- *". . . listened to what we wanted to do. He was able to think of all the options and how to get it done. He presented all options to us which made working with him very easy."*
- *"He designed a bathroom on the third floor of our home. It was very functional and it came out much nicer than we expected."*

 _____
_____
_____

Beer & Coleman, (908)757-7007, A, 10 years in business

Beer & Coleman is widely esteemed for its custom residential designs and its innovative approach to commercial developments. The expert staff of licensed architects take pride in defining the standard of excellence in design consistency, cost-efficiency and quality control. They are committed to maximizing resale values and helping clients to avoid costly and time-consuming mistakes through project management, leadership and professionalism.

- *"They are very personable and enthusiastic. Creative with their work."*
- *". . . sat down with us several times to work through everything until we were completely happy with the design. We would definitely recommend them."*

 _____
_____
_____

Bielecki Architect, (908)722-6830, A, 47 years in business

Mr. Bielecki studied architecture at the Polish School of Architecture in London which was part of London University. His own words best describe his work philosophy: "Architecture is an Art. I consider myself as an artist, but not every architect is an artist. To be an architect-artist one has to be born with talent to recognize beauty, proportions, colors, shapes, sounds, and classical meanings and then to apply it to practical use. I think I am that type of architect-artist. The painter would not paint the same picture many times over. So my designs are like the painter's—each one is different."

- *"Stan Bielecki has handled full plans for the restoration of my historic house which unfortunately was damaged extensively by a fire. He is knowledgeable and professional in every way—retaining the old through the delicate balance of details and also satisfying the new requirements."*

 _____
_____

Alexander A. Bol Architect and Assoc., (908)464-9100, A, 25 years in business

Alexander Bol is a licensed architect and professional planner. He began his career with firms working in urban areas and on large government projects. He has a strong interest in working with the traditional styles that are prevalent in New Jersey. His firm excels at blending the design with the surrounding architecture. Many of his new projects look as if they have been standing for decades. His work on dozens of turn-of-the-century mansions in manyof this state's most prestigious communities has earned him a reputation for quality design of older buildings. One of his most intriguing projects was the development of plans for "Drumthwacket" which is the governor's mansion in Princeton.

- *"In 1985 he designed the addition to our older home. He kept the architecture and feel of the new part in harmony with the older. He did a wonderful job. We enjoyed working with him and absolutely love this room. It is a source of many compliments from our friends."*
- *"When he designs an addition, he makes it look like it has always been on the house or part of the house. His details are to perfection as far as giving the correct architecture appointments to the home."*
- *"Our builder really had an easy time with his plans which was really a plus. Other builders who have worked with him feel the same way. Everything just fell into place. "*
- *"He is known as a restoration architect and he lives by his name. I have an old house and he came up with a new roof line for a kitchen addition which was cleverly done. This comes with experience."*

DeBiasse & Seminara Architects, (908)713-0809, A, 6 years in business

As a residential architect this firm focuses on clear communication with clients to ensure that their needs, desires and ideas are incorporated into the final built environment. Their expertise is space planning, project feasibility, land acquisitions, period architecture design and construction. They pride themselves on looking at the big picture when completing a project, whatever its size, often uncovering new avenues to creative solutions.

- *"Michael DeBiasse has a lot of initiative, energy and new ideas which he brings to all his architectural projects."*

Michael D. Giambalvo Architect, (908)317-5051, A, 15 years in business

This architect is also a general contractor. He will design and build for residential and commercial establishments.

- *"We are in the process of redoing the upstairs of our garage and making it into a recreation area. We would also like to add a two-car garage. He has come very highly recommended to us by friends and we were very impressed with his professionalism and proposals."*

Maxine Giordano Architect, (908)706-5250, MIC, 2 years in business

Maxine is an architect and space planner. She specializes in designing master plans of the home so all work is done in harmony with the customer's needs and surroundings.

- *"The primary reason we used her was that she understood and could translate from 'lay' language into building. She is willing to spend as much time as necessary to make sure the job is perfect."*
- *"She is extremely creative. We had our own ideas but before she agreed to only doing what we thought was right, she wanted to know if we had considered anything else as a possibility. She is very open and has many suggestions. We worked both our ideas together and we came up with a satisfactory solution to our third-floor renovation."*

Klesse Associates, (973)379-6602, UC MC WC, 15 years in business

Klesse Associates is an award-winning design firm specializing in residential projects. Their scope of services includes custom-designed additions, alterations and historic preservation work. The company owner, Timothy P. Klesse, believes in tailoring his design solutions to maintain the integrity of the building while satisfying the client's specific needs. A combination of training in architecture and interior design gives him a thorough insight into the complexities of the modern interior environment.

- *"Tim designed our kitchen. He knocked out the wall to a maid's room and made one big room. He was very sensitive to our ideas and has an eye for detail. He designed a beautiful kitchen. One thing I liked is that he even went with me to shop for cabinets and appliances."*
- *"He designed and worked on an addition to the exterior of our house. He was very careful to maintain the overall architectural theme of the house. He was diligent and worked well with our contractor. A great guy!"*

David M. Rosen Architects, (908)273-6565, UC MC SC, 11 years in business

The fifteen members on the staff of this firm are comprised of architects and designers with experience in a wide range of renovation projects and new construction. The firm has expanded to include commercial, municipal and medical work, while continuing to enjoy long-term relationships with local residents.

- *"I love David! He is a terrific architect. He completely renovated our whole house. I know from just our friends coming into our home he has gotten many referrals. I would use David in a minute again."*
- *"He is very cooperative in following our suggestions. He had no problem when I changed my mind mid-course or there had to be some corrections. He just worked beautifully with the contractor or land designer and we were all always able to*

put our heads together and work out a solution that was best for our home. He is a first-rate architect. I can't say enough nice things about him."

✍ _____
_____
_____

John B. Rubinstein, (973)992-4242, MC SC WC , 22 years in business
This architectural firm spends as much time as needed in the beginning of a project so that the customer's needs are fully understood. A unique, correct solution is then designed for each client. Site visits continue to assure a well-executed finished product.
- *"For that special home there is no one better to work with. He has a wonderful disposition and is extraordinarily talented. He has a very easy way about him. I think his specialty is contemporary homes but he is definitely a man for all seasons."*

✍ _____
_____
_____

Scialla and Associates Architects Inc., (973)543-9669, A, 30 years in business
Bob is a residential architect who has extensive knowledge of almost all facets of architecture and related matters such as: construction, negotiations, space planning, and coordination of all the professions needed to perform effectively in the real estate project setting. He combines the technical expertise of an architect with the management and marketing on the business side.
- *"He is an excellent architect and a wonderful man. He has an easy personality and is so nice to work with."*

✍ _____
_____
_____

Sincox Associates Architects, (908)232-8188, A, 17 years in business
Sincox Architects has worked on many project including such building types as shopping malls, school and daycare facilities, churches, movie theaters, offices, medical facilities and residences. In 1986 they made a full commitment to grow through technology. That year a multistation computer drafting was implemented to assist in considering design options and improve efficiency. Personalized service and growth through technology allow this small firm to compete successfully.
- *"A great guy. We were very pleased working with him. He is very personable and accommodating. Very approachable . . . open to suggestions and listens very carefully."*

✍ _____
_____
_____

Subhas Architects, (908)789-2522, A, 10 years in business
Margaret is a residential architect and interior designer. She specializes in the areas of space planning, additions, new residences and commercial office planning, restaurants and shops.

- *"She's a good architect and designer. She's great with exterior design and matching existing structures."*
- *"She's responsible and gets along easily with both customers and contractors."*

✍️ _____

_____

_____

Hiland Hall Turner Assoc. Architects, (908)719-2020, A, 8 years in business

With offices in New York and Far Hills the staff of this firm offers personalized service. The firm has experience with major alterations and additions to a variety of types and styles of residences throughout the tri-state area. A great deal of emphasis is placed on the predesign process and Mr. Turner feels that he's "not only designing a home for myself, so I need to determine how my clients live, what their aesthetic concerns are and how they view the built environment." Often he accompanies clients to the building site to examine how the home should relate to its surroundings.

- *"Hiland Turner has many faces—designer, artist, architect. But most important he is a listener. After asking his client what kind of environment they want to create, he listens to the many half-expressed ideas, stitching them together in his mind until some creative threshold is reached. Then like a kid reacting to a newly discovered toy, he will explode with ideas. 'What would you think if we . . .' If you are dissatisfied with the rectangular monotony of your current ranch house, he will suggest additions that add softening curves. It you want to create a new room that blurs the distinction between indoors and outdoors, he will invoke new space with high ceilings and walls filled with apparently boundless windows. His architectural solutions have a novel twist—a dash of unexpected. Working with Hiland Turner is an adventure. If you can imagine the sensation of living in your dream house, he can create the structure to make your feelings an enduring reality."*

✍️ _____

_____

_____

Vincentsen Associates, (908)232-4642, A, 10 years in business

Architecture and planning for residences, churches and schools are the specialities of Barbara Vincentsen.

- *"We were very happy with her work. We blew out the top part of our house and she came up with the concept for our new master bedroom and bathroom. She did a really nice job."*
- *"She designed our kitchen addition and renovation. We actually went through a couple of architects before deciding on Barbara—we liked her best. She's very practical—made it functional as well as good-looking. She is also a mother and a cook, so she has a sense of not doing stupid things just to make it look nice."*
- *"She is professional and competent. Barbara and her group did a terrific job on the plans for my kitchen. I appreciated her professionalism and personal touch."*

✍️ _____

_____

VJM Architecture, (908)781-1676, SC, 8 years in business

VJM Architecture offers homeowners the highest quality architectural design services from the initial consultation to the successful completion of construction. The owner, Jim Matarazzo, prides himself on his ability to listen to the needs and ideas of his clients and incorporate them into each project. By using the latest in computer-aided design equipment, VJM has created a number of unique home designs from which builders and home buyers can choose.

- *"He comes up with unique and different plans. He will include a lot of nice architectural details. He is very detail-conscious and very professional. He's a well-rounded architect."*
- *"He is very friendly and easy to work with. His plans are always well thought-out and he comes up with ideas we would never have thought of. He has a great reputation. I really like this guy."*

Yarrington Architectural Group, (908)526-2222, A, 14 years in business

This architectural firm gives personalized attention to their clients' goals. They specialize in residential renovations, additions and building new homes.

- *"We chose Mark primarily because he was very easy to work with and very personable. He was willing to listen to our ideas and he had great ideas. He was flexible in terms of our wants. We were very comfortable with him and are pleased with the results."*

CARPENTERS

Authorized Alterations, Inc., (732)656-1460, UC SC MIC, 7 years in business

Authorized Alterations provides all aspects of quality home improvement services including kitchens, baths, decks, roofing, siding, additions, windows and doors. Areas of specialization are custom kitchens and bathrooms.

- *". . . very talented craftsmen. We have had several small carpentry jobs that we knew a contractor would not want to do. Authorized Alterations tackled each job and we were so pleased with the results."*
- *"They are so pleasant and want to please the customer."*

Wayne Bizup Builders, (908)756-6468, MIC, 21 years in business

Many of Wayne Bizup's customers compile "odd job" lists of small, miscellaneous repairs for this talented carpenter. His special expertise is bathroom remodeling.

- *"I have known him for 25 years. He started as a teenager doing odd jobs."*
- *"I trust him implicitly. He's very knowledgeable."*

Ronald F. Brooks Carpentry and Home Improvements, (732)985-1194, UC SC MIC, 14 years in business

All work for this carpentry and home improvement business is done by the owner. Areas of concentration include kitchens, bathrooms, basements, windows, doors, decks and interior and exterior repairs. He prides himself on returning calls promptly and quotes are given within three days of viewing a job.

- *"A fine young man with integrity and talent."*
- *"Have used him for small jobs but know he is capable for much larger."*
- *"Did exactly what I had requested. He's the kind of person you would like to have as a son."*

Cedarcreek Construction , (908)561-0286, UC SC MC WC, 20 years in business

Mark Russo, the owner of Cedarcreek Construction has worked with his father since he was 15 years old. Whatever odd carpentry jobs there are, Mark is willing to do them. Although he calls himself a general carpenter, areas of expertise include kitchens, bathrooms, wall units, cabinets, sheet rock patching and Formica tops.

- *"He was recommended by a friend—I saw the job he did in her kitchen and decided to use him."*
- *"I trust him when I am not at home."*
- *"He takes pride in his work."*

- *"He did French doors between the dining and living room—it looks like they have always been there."*

✍ _____

_____

_____

Joey Chapurtinov Carpentry, Inc., (732)919-0345, UC MIC, 20 years in business
Attention to detail and quality are hallmarks of this carpenter's work. All general construction with an emphasis on remodeling and renovation are done. Areas of expertise include carpentry, custom woodworking and interior custom trim.
- *"He's a very detail-oriented person—punctual, neat and reliable."*
- *"He's a quiet person—very nice to have around."*

✍ _____

_____

_____

Choice Custom Millwork, Inc., (215)702-1600, A, 8 years in business
An architectural woodworking firm that specializes in custom-built front entryways, raised panel libraries, interior doors, built-ins and furniture replication. They are a self-described "turn-key" operation and will work with the customer to create a unique design suited to the job.
- *". . . does nice detailing with woodwork."*
- *"He did my husband's study and is now custom-building a dining room table for us."*
- *"He made a beautiful vanity for a bathroom in my house. What a nice person!"*

✍ _____

_____

_____

CJC Renovations, Inc., (908)232-4004, A, 10 years in business
Customers who have used CJC Renovations have generally heard about this firm through word-of-mouth since they do no advertising. They provide a complete service in remodeling homes from design to completion. A staff of full-time employees work closely with the customer to provide fast, clean, professional service.
- *"They are very dependable. They do odd jobs that a lot of other people will not do."*
- *"Good restoration work!"*

✍ _____

_____

_____

Custom Woodworking, (908)232-9525, A, 17 years in business
Custom cabinets and millwork is this firm's major business. They create the kind of rooms that their customers enjoy working and living in because they are aesthetically pleasing and functional.
- *"They took out our original screen door and reproduced it detail by detail."*

- *"Beautiful work done by a nice guy."*

_____
_____
_____

E & R Contractors, (732) 574-3681, A, 26 years in business

To the smallest detail all work is meticulously done by this general carpenter. Kitchens, bathrooms and interior remodeling are his major areas of interest.

- *"He's a pleasure to work with. He paid attention to all our needs."*
- *"I would not hesitate to have him back again in my home!"*

_____
_____
_____

Furino Custom Woodwork, (908)534-4511, MC SC MIC, 10 years in business

If you dream it, Furino will make it! This company can custom-build and install anything. The customer is given assistance in designing the project and is continuously consulted through every step of the way.

- *"He listened very carefully to everything we wanted and he got it right!"*
- *"Very detail-oriented and patient about any changes made during progression of work."*

_____
_____

Genualdi Building Company, (908)277-0876, UC, 12 years in business

Rich Genualdi has diversified his business over the years to provide the homeowner a range of work. This minimizes the inconvenience of calling many different tradespeople to complete one job. He does work on renovations, additions, deck construction and kitchens.

- *"He stayed within my budget and managed the job well."*
- *"He did the job as I defined it in a very timely fashion."*

_____
_____

Homaico, (908)439-3394, SC MIC WC, 10 years in business

Homaico is abbreviated from Home Maintenance Company. They offer general maintenance services involving building construction. The list of services includes—but is not limited to—additions, alterations, kitchen, bath and basement remodeling, ceramic and marble tiling, interior and exterior trim work and deck work.

- *"I showed him the porch on an old home that I wanted. He duplicated it right down to the layer of flagstone."*
- *". . . very hard-working—stays with a job until completion."*

_____

JMK Builders Inc., (908)730-8050, A, 14 years in business

This is a "hands-on" contracting firm specializing in building additions. They have built everything from family rooms to bathrooms and decks. They pride themselves on making new construction look like it has been an original part of the house.

- *"Very creative people. They took a very small space and made it into a great living area."*
- *"They do quality work."*

JMK Contractors, (908)245-5263, A, 15 years in business

John Koulouthros is the owner/operator of JMK. This firm does carpentry, additions, painting and tile work.

- *"He is a general contractor, but will also do small odd jobs that no one else seems to want to do. No job is too small for him. I know I can count on him. Everyone can always use a 'John.'"*

Leonardis Architectural Design & Construction, Inc., (908)852-4722, A, 35 years in business

Alfonse Leonardis is an architectural designer with Old-World experience. He prides himself on creating truly unique, romantic settings. Complete design service is available with interior and exterior remodeling, custom baths, kitchens, libraries and wine cellars.

- *"They designed my kitchen. They were extremely patient, took time with every detail and were excellent to work with. The proof is now I have a beautiful kitchen!"*

Lindex Construction Company, (908)756-1455, A, 15 years in business

Workmen that treat your home as if it were their own are a rarity. Lindex Construction handles all aspects of project needs and if they can't perform part of the project they find someone who can. All types of carpentry are done on both new and old homes.

- *"They are very versatile craftsmen."*
- *". . . type of people you can call at 7pm on a Saturday night and they will come immediately to fix whatever it is."*
- *"Impressive remodeling and did a hardwood floor—outstanding!"*

J. Mooney Designs Co., (973)344-2146, A, 20 years in business

As a custom cabinetmaker Jim Mooney designs, constructs and installs with a principal emphasis on built-ins. Emphasis is placed on providing well-executed cabinetry which is functional and stylish while at the same time suited to the architectural surroundings. He renders his own designs after determining the needs of the customer and works closely with customer's designers and/or architects to implement plans.

CARPENTERS

- *"Jim does great, exquisite work. I have used him for five years for all our custom woodwork and cabinets."*
- *"He did a magnificent job on a friend's vanity and that's why we contracted him. He did not disappoint us!"*

Brian Munroe Home Remodeling, (732)560-0472, A, 4 years in business

This small company is willing to take the time to go over what the customer wants and needs and they make sure the job is done right. They remodel kitchens and bathrooms.

- *"Very skilled and excellent carpenter in terms of cabinets, molding, building shelves, finishing door frames to match parts of the existing room. A really nice guy."*

Nalven & Rowe Building & Design, (908)789-1954, UC SC MIC WC, 12 years in business

Peter Nalven and Tom Rowe take pride in doing work that takes a little thought and attention to detail. They will hang a door or build a full addition—serving as designer and contractor. Specialties include additions, kitchens, bathrooms, decks, custom cabinetry in addition to restoration of old structures, Victorian moldings and collapsing porches. They are particularly adept at architectural restoration of old buildings.

- *"They are prompt and dependable."*
- *"We researched by looking at work done by them on old houses and decided that they knew what they were doing. We decided to use their services."*
- *". . . did all our woodwork in our den area. He also built cabinets, put in beams and did a fireplace mantel with columns. He is just wonderful with detailing. One word to describe him is—detailing. He refinishes all of his woodwork so he can oversee everything from start to finish."*

Pakenham Building & Home Improvements, (908)232-3901, UC, 10 years in business

No job is too large or too small for Chip Pakenham. He works on one job at a time from start to finish, so the homeowner receives the ultimate personal touch. He acts as a general contracting service for other professions such as masons, plumbers, etc. Many of these people have been working with him for years.

- *"A real nice guy. He hung doors for me."*
- *"He does good, solid work. He has excellent response time and is a great guy too!"*

Quality Interior Systems & Co., (908)769-1100, A, 21 years in business

As an interior contractor, this firm will do framing and drywall, acoustical ceilings, doors and windows, any interior carpentry work, kitchens and bathrooms. All work is done by the owners from start to finish.

- *"They are impeccable. A perfect name for the business!"*

- *"He transformed our basement into a great recreational family room. He had great suggestions and now we're going to have him do our kitchen."*

✍ _____

_____

Tom Robinson's Carpentry, (732)738-9507, UC MIC, 15 years in business

This carpenter specializes in kitchen renovations, all types of windows and doors and interior trim. All jobs are done solely by Tom Robinson who works closely with the customer and other involved tradespeople to ensure a quality job.
- *"Quick and efficient"*
- *"He cleans up well which we place a great emphasis on."*

✍ _____

_____

Shea Carpentry & Building, (908)654-7226, UC, 14 years in business

This business provides total construction services. They strive for the coordination of fine craftsmanship with the integrity of the existing architecture. As a general contractor, Shea Carpentry oversees all aspects of the job to ensure that architectural and design plans are carried out beautifully.
- *"Joe Shea is very professional. He is totally creative and has a great eye!"*
- *"He did work on my older home when we first moved in . They were small jobs and some plastering. He gets to really know his clients. A wonderful worker, very professional. Really creative and has a good eye."*

✍ _____

_____

Toddco Construction, (973)376-5889, A, 10 years in business

Toddco is a small contracting company that does everything from home renovations to small home repairs. They are a perfect-sized firm to provide very personalized service.
- *"He built a unit for me in the basement and also a computer table which he covered in Formica that I chose. This unit was completely custom. Whatever we asked him to do he did. He did a lovely job."*

✍ _____

_____

CATERERS

Best Darn Foods, (732)899-6398, A, 12 years in business
Gourmet soup and dip mixes are made by the two female owners. Their apple crisp was recommended by Joan Hamburg and John Gambling on WOR radio. All products are original recipes, attractively packaged and have natural ingredients with no added salt.
- *"Last winter my husband and I were craving soup and I ordered one of their soup mixes (Soup from the Coop). It reminded me of my grandmother's chicken soup. It was a wonderful surprise and we immediately ordered some more."*
- *"Their apple crisp is to die for."*

Catering Productions, Inc., (201)652-1682, A, 12 years in business
Catering Productions combines the latest trends in food with skillful event coordination. They have the unique ability to incorporate the clients'distinctive visions with their creative expertise which they feel sets them apart from the ordinary.
- *"I had the good fortune of participating in an event catered by this group. The food that was passed was so artistically presented that the guests were reluctant to mess up the trays. Luckily the hors d'oeuvres tasted as good as they looked. Very impressive."*
- *"She is extremely pleasant, not haughty, and easy to work with. So creative."*

Celsos Caterers, (973)829-1833, A, 10 years in business
This chef/caterer specializes in home tented weddings and other social parties.Celsos makes a point of customizing each menu in order to meet the specific tastes and budget of each client. They provide complete event planning including floral arrangements, music, tents and rentals.
- *"The food is delicious and presented tastefully."*
- *"They did a bar mitzvah and it was wonderful. The best thing though was that the food that was supposed to be hot was hot. Sometimes that is not true with caterers."*

Civile Ristorante Italiano/Caterer, (908)709-1155, A, 8 years in business
Civile offers a complete catering service. They will arrange an affair completely from flowers to rentals, special ice carvings and theme settings. Every detail is handled personally by the owner. The staff is trained to be professional and courteous and will create an elegant setting, where needed, yet make the guests feel comfortable. Cuisine is prepared by experienced chefs who pay special attention to detail and take pride in the presentation, flavoring and freshness of all foods.

- *"Sophisticated food and presentation."*
- *"I wish I had found them years ago. He offers very personal attention and their food goes beyond delicious."*

Clyne & Murphy, Inc., (908)233-9733, A, 12 years in business
This catering company offers personal service for planning the perfect party reception or event so that the client can enjoy guests and leave the worries elsewhere. All their food is homemade with the highest quality ingredients. They "sweat the details" so you don't have to.
- *"Extremely friendly. They can handle any size crowd. They prepare their own recipes, but should you furnish them with your own recipe, they will prepare that also. The food is always delicious."*
- *"A terrific team. They have a wide array of items on the menu that you can choose from. They will do a party from beginning to end or just prepare the food and deliver it. Any party that I have had or been to that they have catered has always been good and their food is delicious."*
- *"The staff is always pleasant and professional."*

Laurence Craig Distinctive Catering and Event Management, (973)761-0190, A, 2 years in business
The corporate and social client list from Laurence Craig reads like a Who's Who of movers and shakers. They include Nordstrom, Neiman Marcus, Bloomingdales, The Morris Museum, and the governor of New Jersey. Their specialty is custom menu and party design which reflects the individual personality of the host. Delicious beautifully presented cuisine coupled with precise service continually bring rave reviews from clients. In addition to food and service, they have an in-house floral designer, wedding consultant and location referral service. They will refer entertainment, decorators, valet parking and any other service connected with fine entertaining.
- *"We haven't actually used them but I attended a luncheon they catered and I have never seen anything so spectacular. The food was so unique and different in texture and taste. The table settings were beautiful. The dessert table was set up with mirrors behind so that the desserts were reflected in the mirrors. For our next party I would reach out and use them in a heartbeat."*

Extreme Cuisine, Inc., (908)322-2963, UC, 2 years in business
This young catering company offers a diverse menu of different ethnic cuisine. They place a strong emphasis on the visual as well as the flavorful qualities. They will cater everything from a backyard barbeque to a full-service, white-glove dinner.
- *"Good quality, fresh, delicious food."*
- *"They have done two parties for us and people wanted their cards. They are a very nice family to work with."*

Fine Ingredients, Inc., (800)522-1650, A, 2 years in business

Italian-style biscotti and chocolate-chip cookies are the handmade specialties of Fine Ingredients. They are packaged in beautiful tins or gift boxes. They will also make cookie platters and beautiful, creative favors for any event.

- *"Her homemade cookies and biscotti are scrumptious. Last Christmas I had a dessert party and served Fine Ingredients delights. Everyone loved them and some of my friends followed up because they asked for her phone number."*
- *"She is very accommodating to the customer and a nice person to know. She puts her all into this business and takes it very seriously. And it shows!"*

Gitane Catering Magnifique, (908)518-0120, A, 12 years in business

Catering Magnifique has two divisions—Gitane and Grand Productions. Grand Productions handles all Kosher events and Gitane takes care of all other catering. They handle everything from six- to eight-person dinner parties to 500–1000 person events. All holiday celebrations are catered either with staff or as drop-off. Alan Dennis, the owner, was trained at the Culinary Institue of America and has been a chef in France and all over the U.S. In his words: "The most important thing is that we like what we do."

- *"They are very good. Very reliable."*
- *"He is wonderful to work with. He wants to please the customer at all times. His staff is fantastic, wonderful, great! The food is delicious."*

Min Goldblatt & Sons, Caterers, (908)925-3869, A, 28 years in business

Min Goldblatt specializes in Kosher catering. Every menu is custom-designed to fulfill the unique needs and tastes of the party giver. Their many years of experience, attention to detail, professional staff, elegant cuisine and total coordination of all aspects of the party results in a truly memorable special event. Specially trained chefs have the ability to prepare delicious foods of all types at any location.

- *"Min Goldblatt's food is delicious, wonderful . . . excellent."*
- *"They do lovely presentation . He's a hands-on guy and a real nice person."*
- *"Easy to work with. They stayed at our party the entire time. The wait staff is efficient and professional."*

In Good Taste, (973)379-1920, UC MC, 15 years in business

In Good Taste offers custom catering which includes menu selection, full rental service and service staff for all types of events.

- *"We have used him a bunch of times for catered parties in our home. He's very nice and reliable. He will supply glassware, tables, chairs, coffeepots, etc. He will determine your needs and his food is great."*

J & M Catering, (908)232-0402, A, 28 years in business

All food is prepared the day of the function by this caterer using only the freshest ingredients. The chefs are culinary school graduates with many years of experience. Complete party planning and rentals are available.

- *"They catered my son's graduation party. The food was very good and their staff was fabulous. They even mopped my kitchen floor before they left."*
- *"When we used them they made more than enough food—it was all delicious. I would definitely use them again."*

Joyfull Occassions, (908)273-3917, UC MC SC, 13 years in business

"You eat with your eyes" sums up the philosophy of Joyfull Occassions. The emphasis is on elegant food and beautiful presentations. The needs of the client are taken into consideration when planning an event.

- *"We attended an outdoor garden engagement party that was catered by this group. The food was beautifully presented and tasted wonderful. Everything was so creative—we were tasting combinations I would never have thought would go together and they were fabulous."*
- *"Second only to their food is the staff. They are all very professional and so easy to work with. We were so pleased when they catered a party for us."*

Kadel & Co. Catering, (732)805-0906, A, 9 years in business

Kadel puts a tremendous amount of love into each affair. They are a full-service catering firm and will also provide rentals and lots of advice.

- *"They catered an engagement party in our home. They were extremely, extremely neat and clean and the food is wonderful."*
- *"They catered a small party at home and everything was wonderful. Our guests made wonderful compliments about the food."*

Mattson & Massaro, Inc., (908)754-6574, A, 7 years in business

Mattson & Massaro does not have a set menu. They say they specialize in "catering to your taste" because they sit down and craft a menu that meets the customer's needs, budget and taste. A list of ideas is presented to the customer and together an individualized plan is crafted. They promise that your party will never be like everybody else's.

- *"M & M has done small and large parties for me. The food is always fabulous. People just eat & eat."*
- *"Their food is always right on target as expected. They are so accommodating and their service is superb. Everything is beautifully done and presented."*
- *"I personally have not used them, however, I have tasted their food at my neighbor's party and it was wonderful. Their presentation is fabulous."*

Monterey Gourmet Shops, Inc, (908)766-2000, A, 9 years in business

Monterey Gourmet feels that they have become synonymous with quality. Quality ingredients, meticulous preparation, high standards of culinary excellence and elegant presentation are what set them apart.

- *"Their hors d'oeuvres are out of this world—particularly their mushroom-leek canapes."*
- *"They are truly wonderful people to work with. Whenever we have a party my good friends will always ask if Monterey Gourmet is catering."*

Not By Bread Alone, (908)464-3345, A, 15 years in business

This company specializes in home events, both large and small. They offer a wide selection of handmade hors d'oeuvres and fresh American-style food. Emphasis is placed on service and each menu is individually planned to meet the customers' needs and preferences. Presentation and attention to detail are the most important components.

- *"Their trays are very attractive. They make use of fresh flowers."*
- *"A really neat staff—professional. They have excellent food and an extensive menu."*

OME Caterers, (973)560-4540, A, 14 years in business

OME caters for the client's social and corporate needs including weddings, bar and bat mitzvahs, graduations, birthdays or anything worth celebrating. Complete event planning, floral arrangements, entertainment and rentals are also available.

- *"We recently attended an at-home wedding that they catered. Their platter design was very pleasing to the eye and also to the palette. They had a highly professional staff and they were very appropriately dressed."*

Soiree Catering, (732)295-1906, A, 15 years in business

This well-established full-service caterer boasts an experienced professional staff of cooks, servers and bartenders. They specialize in gourmet dinners, cocktail parties, luncheons and special personal events. They will also cater informal barbecues and their famous "Classic Clambake." Other services include an experienced party planner to assist the customer with rentals, decorations, and entertainment. All that is left for the party giver to do is to sit back and relax and enjoy your "Soiree."

- *"They are the most notable caterers in my area. Most people I know use them. They always do a marvelous job."*
- *"When you use their services, you can be assured that there will be no worries."*

Sandy Spector Caterer, (908)756-0310, A, 23 years in business

This full-service caterer can take care of all the client's needs from tenting, dance floors, tables, chairs and specialty linens to entertainment, individually designed decor, flowers, staff and everything that goes into making an event special. All food is prepared in their kitchens using no frozen or prepared appetizers, entrees or desserts. They use only the freshest seasonal produce and import a myriad of incredible specialty items. The staff is professionally trained, courteous and they treat each client as if they were their first.

- *"Very pleasant and quite creative. She will work with you to come up with a menu of foods you enjoy. She's very detail-oriented and does lovely presentations. She will match her serving pieces to the decor of your home. "*
- *"Her help is professional, polite and nicely dressed. This is a top-notch operation down to the cleanup. My kitchen was perfect when they left. I have only good words for her."*
- *"She had done huge parties and small, informal parties for us. Her presentation is outstanding. The variety of her menu is very extensive. She has also done our business luncheons and we are never disappointed."*
- *"High quality. She caters at my home every Christmas. We love her."*

Town Square Katering, (908)598-9500, A, 10 years in business
The owners of this catering company are graduates of the Culinary Institute of America. They do off-premise catering for events from 2 to 5000 people.

- *"All our parties at home have been catered by Town Square. They catered a 50th birthday party for my husband which was a huge success. It was outside on our patio. They have efficient service and the staff are really great people."*
- *"Their food is amazingly delicious and the presentation is lovely. They will also work with you on table decorations, linens and flowers.*

Wickey's Caterers, (800)WICKEY-1, A, 18 years in business
"Great events begin with Wickey's." With years of hands-on catering and event planning and management experience, they feel they can create your great event. They offer a fully trained professional staff, bar attendants with "TIPS" safety program certification and valet service. In addition they provide artistically designed menus, eye-catching table appointments, specialty linens, rental equipment, floral services and additional event planning services. Most of all they provide "peace of mind."

- *"They have catered two weddings at our home. People are still giving me compliments on the creativity and quality of the food."*
- *"I would say he's just tops. There are caterers and there is Wickey's. Out of all the recommendations I gave you for this book, he is the most extraordinary."*

CHIMNEYS

Afton Contractors, (973)635-1460, MC, 35 years in business

Afton concentrates on chimneys. They will rebuild and repair chimneys, remove pests, correct furnace violations and clean fireplaces.

- *"I called him on a Monday and on Wednesday he was at my home cleaning my chimney. I feel that was definitely timely service."*
- *"He has a lot of experience and did a good job. He cleaned up thoroughly. Very pleasant."*

Bogard's Solid Flue Inc. T/A Chimney savers, (800)336-5688, UC MIC, 14 years in business

Bogard's SolidFlue is a unique chimney lining system ideally suited to reline and restore old, damaged or worn out chimney flues. This is a small business consisting of three highly skilled workers. It has been recognized as Installer of the Year in 1990, 1994 and 1996 for high-quality workmanship and customer relations.

- *"They replaced our chimney flues. They were very professional and were extremely neat and clean."*

Chimney Savers, (908)359-7798, MC SC WC, 13 years in business

With Chimney Savers the customer can get a complete chimney restoration, change in size, style and brick color. They also provide a complete line of insurance work from lightning damage to chimney fire damage. They will also replace terra-cotta tile that has been damaged with Solid Flue™ a stainless steel liner.

- *"They are very, very good! They are the most professional and best workers I have had in my home. They replaced and relined chimneys in my home. They covered everything with plastic and there was not a speck of dirt when they left."*

Crown Sweep Inc., (908)866-1666, A, 12 years in business

This is a full chimney service which includes chimney sweeping, repairs, flashing, interior and exterior bricks, caps, screens and waterproofing.

- *"Good job. They were very reliable. They repaired the back of the firebox.*
- *"They repaired the top of the chimney and installed a chimney cover. They cleaned our chimneys. They are our chimney people and we continue to use them over and over."*

David the Village Sweep, (908)756-1807, UC SC, 18 years in business

In addition to providing a high level of expertise in chimney maintenance and use, this company focuses on customer service—courtesy, prompt return of calls, on-time arrival, honest evaluations, spotless work, computerized service records and follow-up calls. They publish a newsletter, mailed free to all customers, which contains great tips on fireplace use, safety, and hazards to avoid.

- *"He's wonderful. Meticulously clean—covers my rugs and furniture. He is extremely careful with our possessions."*
- *"He will not clean your chimney if he feels it does not need to be cleaned. He will offer many wonderful suggestions (such as capping). We were very pleased with his service."*

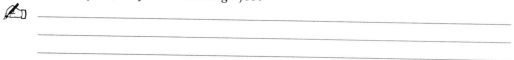

Home Energy Conservation, (908)754-5750, UC MC SC MIC, 18 years in business

Home Energy specializes in cleaning woodstoves, chimneys and fireplaces. They will also install inserts and reline. In addition to their service work they have a showroom where the customer can view stoves, fireplaces and accessories.

- *"As a homeowner and being somewhat in the chimney business, what is great about Home Energy is that they are good and honest. The customer really has no way of knowing what is inside his chimney which is why he has a professional come in. Home Energy will not clean your chimney if you don't need it. And when they do, they do a thorough job."*

Kringle's Chimney Sweep, Ltd., (800)651-KRIS, MC SC WC, 1 year in business

The owners of Kringle's feel that their efforts to educate and make the homeowner and general public aware of the serious health risks from carbon monoxide poisoning and the real danger of fire and property loss due to improperly built and maintained chimneys sets them apart from other chimney sweeps. They will install and maintain chimneys, woodstoves, furnaces and even dryer vents.

- *"He has cleaned all six of our chimneys. Mike is great. He's neat, clean, moved whatever furniture he had to and put it back in place."*
- *"He inspected all our fireplaces and was honest about it. He described which ones should be taken care of and which ones not. He is a great find."*

McPuff Chimney Sweep, (908)806-2389, UC MC SC MIC, 20 years in business

McPuff Chimney offers a variety of services including: cleaning of fireplaces, oil and gas furnace flues, woodstoves and woodstove inserts. They also do chimney repairs, chimney caps and chimney relining.

- *"They are very accommodating. They did a good job cleaning and made general suggestions about the upkeep of the chimney. They will handle such things as removal of dead animals that are stuck in the chimney."*

✍ _____
_____
_____

Puffin Chimney Service, Inc. , (732)249-6886, SC MIC, 3 years in business
"Chimney safety: It isn't just for fireplaces." So says this female owner/operator of Puffin. She treats each home as if it were her own by sweeping the fireplace and woodstove chimneys. She performs evaluations required for condo associations and prebuy or sale evaluations on homes. Other services include installing chimney caps, removing animals, unblocking chimneys, masonry repairs,waterproofing, relining.

- *". . . a chimney cleaning service that does a meticulous, wonderful job."*
- *"She is so reliable and punctual. You hardly know when she's in the house."*

✍ _____
_____
_____

CHINA & CRYSTAL REPAIR

Glass Restorations, (212)517-3287, A, 30 years in business

If you have broken that priceless or not so priceless crystal or china piece, Glass Restorations can repair it. They specialize in Baccarat, Daum, Lalique, Steuben, Waterford, and all antique and contemporary glass.

- *"During a move the only thing that broke was an antique crystal candle sconce that belonged to my grandmother. It was seriously damaged. I actually had several people look at it and they all said it was beyond hope—that is until I found Augustine, the owner of Glass Restorations. He was able to find a piece that he could use to replace the broken piece. He also knew someone who was able to make a metal base. I was so pleased that I could resusctitate something that I loved. He did a wonderful job. Expert work!"*

Hess Restorations, (212)360-6211, A, 52 years in business

Hess will repair and restore objects of art such as china, ceramics, wood, ivory, and crystal. All work is done by European-trained restorers. They restore both decorative and utilitarian objects and will grind chips on crystal glasses.

- *"They repaired a broken antique Victorian berry bowl which was my grandmother's. Did a beautiful job. They take care and are meticulous in craftsmanship."*
- *"They repaired a dish that I had broken and repaired it to perfection. They do fine restoration of anything of value and I was very impreseed when I finally saw their operation."*

Restorations by Dudley Inc., (973)731-4449, A, 16 years in business

Dudley is a professional self-taught restorer of fine porcelain and figurines. His specialities include: restoration of figurines, statuettes, Hummels, Lladro, Royal Doulton, Dresden, Meissen and Boehm. Over the years he has developed many techniques such as: the fabrication of missing parts, noses, fingers, toes, etc. He has developed special glazes and finishes which are applied by airbrush.

- *"He repaired a Lladro figurine in which a portion of the hand was broken. When he returned it to me there was no way of telling that it was worked on. "*
- *"Dudley is an absolute treasure to find and hold on to."*

CHINA & CRYSTAL REPAIR

Stephenson's Inc., (732)223-2818, A, 12 years in business

Stephen Weston's work is the combination of artistry and restorationist. His results are like a work of art. He will restore fine porcelain such as Connoisseur, Cybis and Boehm. He does work for galleries around the country as well as for private people.

- *"He does beautiful porcelain restoration. He cleaned my Cybis porcelain and repaired our Connoisseru of Malvern. An orchid petal broke off—and you would never know there was a repair on it. "*
- *"He cleaned all my porcelain and has repaired pieces of antique chine—fine china. You cannot tell that they were repaired."*

CLOCK REPAIR

Antique Clock Gallery, (908)534-6070, A, 20 years in business
This small family business offers a very personal touch—handcrafting and handling the fine timepieces from years gone by. They are able to offer top quality restoration, conservation methods on movements as well as the total clock.

- *"I purchased a beautiful antique clock from them. We hung it up over our fireplace, not on a great hook. It fell off and broke into a million pieces. They were able to repair it and get it working again. You cannot see where the repairs are and I am absolutely amazed."*
- *"They repaired a grandfather's clock for me. They are extremely nice people to deal with."*

The Chester Timepiece, (908)879-5421, MC SC WC, 18 years in business
Chester Timepiece specializes in repairing keywind, wall and mantel clocks. They will make house calls and will also set up and offer packing for clocks.

- *"We were very pleased with the way they repaired our antique clock. They came to the house, were very pleasant and knew exactly what they were doing. I would use them again."*

Country Clock Works, (800)853-4244, A, 15 years in business
This business is a little different because they try to offer as much help as possible on the phone. If need be, they will come to the home. They will take the time to call their regular customers every day to see if they need help regulating their clocks and to resolve problems. They go a long way to please customers and do not consider phone calls to be a bother.

- *"When we moved into our home, they moved our grandfather's clock, wrapped it carefully, delivered it, set it up and serviced it. They did a beautiful job."*
- *"They fixed a mantel clock. They're very nice to work with and really did take good care of our clock."*

Eva's Corner, (973)779-4334, A, 26 years in business
With this many years of experience, Eva's Corner can repair any type of clock. If you need repair on tall case or grandfather's clock they will certainly come to your home.

- *"They are very good. They have repaired my grandfather's clock and a few other clocks. They get the job done in a reasonable amount of time and are reliable."*

Gordin & Sons, (908)232-0736, UC, 18 years in business

The Gordins will repair and take care of that special clock in your home whether it be antique or new.

- *"I purchased an antique clock that did not work at all. They fixed it and I have had no problems since. I was very pleased with their level of expertise in clock repair."*

_____
_____
_____

The Pendulum, Inc., (908)722-0447, SC, 3 years in business

This business specializes in repair and restoration of fine clocks. Housecalls are made to assess damage and repair costs.

- *"He does excellent repairs. He is very knowledgeable and reputable. He's extremely honest."*

_____
_____
_____

Frank Snyder Antique Clocks, (908)464-0516, A, 25 years in business

Frank Snyder is known for restoration of antique music clocks, Black Forest restorations on flute-playing clocks and fine antique French, German and English clocks. All antique replacement parts are handmade. A pick-up and delivery service is provided.

- *"He specializes in cuckoo clocks and there aren't too many people around that do. He can fix any kind of clock. He's wonderful."*
- *"He has a wonderful clock collection, so he just delights in seeing old clocks."*

_____
_____
_____

CLOSETS

California Closets, (973)882-3800, A, 13 years in business

This franchise in Fairfield has been owned and successfully operated by the same family for 13 years. They are proud of their reputation for customer service and on-time installation of high quality storage systems. They will provide California Closets–custom designs for closets, home offices, garages, pantries, laundry rooms and the entire home.

- *"They spent a long time consulting with me regarding my needs and ideas. They do an accurate count and measurement of all our personal clothing articles in the closet."*
- *"Extremely innovative. They give you the benefit of their expertise and make good suggestions. The installation was fast and relatively cheap. The end product was extremely functional. They will come back at any time if you want adjustments for they feel it is important that you live with it for awhile."*
- *"When we did a major renovation on our home, they did every single closet. They are reliable and we are very happy with all the closets they installed for they did the job exactly as they said they would."*

Closet Experts, (973)366-3022, A, 13 years in business

Closet Experts will design and install to maximize your space. They are not a franchise and they work on a one-day basis. They will design closets, garages, home offices and more. Photos of previous jobs can be shown.

- *"If you want instant gratification Closet Experts is for you! They will organize your closets within hours. Their practical expertise is why I have used and reused them over the years."*

The Closet Factory, (800)720-8270, A, 12 years in business

Whether you are looking for a sturdy budget material, standard or custom laminates or beautiful hardwoods and veneers, The Closet Factory can provide them all. Their professional staff of personal space planners is trained to design your closet to fit you and your lifestyle. The entire system is manufactured in their own factory. They will customize with accessories including racks and drawers to hold ties, belts, jewelry, cedar, baskets, mirrors, hampers, ironing boards, lucite doors, shoe cubbies and more. Shelf stability and full adjustability is assured by state-of-the-art drilling equipment.

- *"My closets looked like the "before" picture in ads for closet companies. The saleswoman for Closet Factory redesigned all my closets to fit each specific need such as my teenage daughters, my sloppy husband, etc. We're thrilled with the imposed level of organization and I'm sure it will help when we decide to sell our house."*

Closet Suppliers Inc., (973)824-1335, UC MC SC MIC, 20 years in business

Closet Suppliers will design and install Melamine and wire shelving systems by Schulte. They feature the "True Space" storage system.

- *"We built a new home and they did all our closets. It's so nice to have such organization. They listened to all my needs."*
- *"It was such an easy job and painless that I don't even remember what the installer looked like!"*

 _____

_____

_____

Creative Closets Ltd., (800)222-4464, A, 13 years in business

Creative Closets specializes in organizing any type of storage area whether it be in your home or office. They will install a built-in closets in children's rooms as well as home-office centers. The two newest additions to their presentations are Murphy beds and total garage systems using adjustable wall systems. Whether it be your master closet, pantry, laundry room, garage or office, "The Closet Lady" can help.

- *"They did exactly what I wanted. They did not try to sell me on any ideas. They're not pushy."*
- *"They're fast, efficient and clean."*

_____

_____

_____

Boise Office Equipment Inc., (908)755-5544, A, 18 years in business

The service technicians at Boise can diagnose any problem the customer may have with computers. They offer sales and service of Apple and Compaq micro computers.

- *"Honest. They always give a fair opinion of the problem. We have used them for maintenance for years."*
- *"They are the only people I know that can fix a MAC within a reasonable amount of time."*

Brennan Consulting, (732)449-6619, UC MIC, 12 years in business

Gail Brennan is an experienced professional computer trainer. She generally trains in the customer's home and is skilled in automation and all Windows applications.

- *"I went from being computer illiterate to being computer literate thanks to Gail. Several of my friends have taken courses from her and they feel that she taught them well."*

Burke Computer Services, (908)412-0520, UC SC MIC, 1 year in business

Terry Burke will sell desktops, mobile computers and peripherals. He also provides an upgrade and repair service. As a consultant, he will also design and install software based on the customer's requirements.

- *"This guy is great! He has a wonderful personality and he has the patience of Job. He is extremely responsive—gets back to you within a matter of hours. I know that he is extremely honest."*
- *"Terry designed our computer database. He ironed out all the glitches and worked well training me to use it. He's very knowledgeable and very patient."*

Computer Net, (888)980-7282, A, 2 years in business

The Computer Net group will sell and service computers. In addition, theywill install and maintain Windows NT and Novell networks.

- *"We bought our computer from them. They are very knowledgeable and helped us to understand what would be suited for us. They set up all our software systems."*

Computer Plus Institute, (973)772-7150, A, 2 years in business

This company offers at-home training in Microsoft applications, Microsoft Windows NT, and Novell Netware. Their instructors are highly qualified, experienced and certified by Microsoft and Novell.

- *"They came to my house and trained both my son and me on our new computer.*

My son, of course, already had experience with computers from school. But I was another story. It was very scary for me, but they were patient and now I feel so comfortable. I e-mail my son at college—no sweat."

DATA deTECHtive, (908)754-1932, UC SC, 10 years in business

Marian Grandolfo, the Data DeTECHtive, does computer consulting and instruction. Her areas of expertise are: software applications including Windows, word processors, publishers and graphics, database management, on-line software and services, financial management and spreadsheets. She will train in the customer's home.

- *"When you buy a new computer and don't know where to begin, Marian is the person to call. She has really helped me with wonderful ideas on how to store and do back-up, etc."*
- *" She is so pleasant. Very nice and dependable. She's a really neat gal."*

Bill Delaney, (908)276-9272, UC, 25 years in business

Bill will train new or not so new computer users as well as those that need help getting started in word processing, spreadsheet, Windows 95,Word 97 and the like. He works real well with baby boomers who did not necessarily grow up with computers.

- *"Bill trained us soon after we bought our computer. We were really novices and in a nice, pleasant, nonthreatening way he brought us into the 20th-century world of computers."*

The Family Computer, (908)508-0570, UC MC SC, 3 years in business

Judy Jacobson works one-on-one in the customer's home. She teaches her clients to use their software and helps them choose and purchase the right system for their needs and budget. She will adapt and upgrade family computers to easily accommodate children.

- *"She's very knowledgeable about computer hardware and software. A very bright person. She works with you to help design a system that's right for you and the family."*
- *"She really knows software and loves what she does. She is a really good listener and is dedicated to do a good job."*

PC Discovery Center, (973)635-2202, UC MC, 3 years in business

PC Discovery will train kids and adults on the computer. They offer multimedia education and Microsoft Office training for adults.

- *"I am 80 years old. I decided before I leave this earth that I am going to buy a computer and learn how to use it. Long story short there was something wrong with my computer and Susan at PC Discovery found it. She spoke with the company and within two days I received a new computer. Susan gave me lessons on how to use it. I found her very pleasant and knowledgeable."*

- *"I learned a lot from Susan and Lea during the private lessons on my computer at home. They have wonderful teaching skills for the beginner, intermediate and advanced user. They are very thorough and easy to work with."*

RMS Computer Solutions, (800)994-4844, MC SC, 5 years in business

RMS offers customized instruction, from stand-alone personal computers to multiuser systems and networks. They are experienced professionals, professionally trained with resources that enable them to answer almost any general support question and to provide troubleshooting expertise. They will also provide product repairs. Their area of expertise is with: IBM, Performa, Macintosh computers, DOS, Windows 3.1, 3.11, 95, Apple Operating Systems, business applications, word processing, spreadsheets and accounting.

- *"In my more computer-naive days, they helped me install new equipment. Now with a boost from them I am more independent. They have recommended suitable hardware and software and provided me with a good level of support."*

Vigilant Computers, (732)381-9528, UC MC SC MIC, 4 years in business

Vigilant will not only sell and service your computer but they will provide training and most of all hand-holding. They make sure their customers are totally comfortable with their systems.

- *"He builds computers. He knows everything there is to know. He built a computer for my husband's waiting room in his pediatric practice for the children to use. After he did this project and we thought he did a wonderful job, he then came to our home and rebuilt a computer with speakers, CD-ROM and fax. He can take any computer and completely update it. He's wonderful!"*

W.B.D. Data Processing Services, (908)889-6551, UC WC, 7 years in business

Bill Dietze will offer individual one-on-one training in your home or place of business. With seven years of personal computer experience and 20 years of data processing he will also provide training of Microsoft products, Windows 95, Microsoft Word and Microsoft Excel.

- *"He is the nicest person and he really knows computers. He is extremely reliable and trustworthy. When we purchased our new computer, Bill got it up and running and taught my husband all he needed to know."*

COMPUTERS

DECORATIVE LIGHTING

Vernon Daniel Associates Landscape Illumination, (973)428-9106, UC MC SC, 30+ years in business
This company specializes in "moonlight illumination" for finer residential properties. They eliminate harsh, glaring floodlights and produce a very sophisticated and romantic moonlit night scene. They approach each property individually and highlight special features and focal points.

- *"They lit our driveway and installed accent lighting for the front of our house. It looks so natural—almost like moonlight. It's a very soft look."*
- *"They have their own electricians who were extemely careful and did not ruin our landscaping while digging. Everything was replaced the way it originally was."*
- *"When they did our landscape lighting, there were portions of certain areas that they had to do touch-up painting. This was done to perfection. We were really pleased with their work."*

Robert Newell Lighting Design, (908)654-9304, A, 14 years in business
Homeowners or their designers are consulted by Robert Newell about lighting design for all types of installations from traditional to contemporary. He will design for both interior and exterior installations.

- *"He installed outdoor lighting in our backyard. We needed to have several trees and bushes illuminated. He gave us advice on creative lighting and I can't tell you how pleased we are that we did this. It has made such a difference."*

George M. Paul Inc., (732)636-9490, UC MIC, 30+ years in business
George is a certified lighting consultant located in the same area for over 30 years. As an electrical contractor, he will install landscape lighting, architectural lighting and do interior lighting design.

- *"He is the only electrician I have used for 21 years. He updated High Hats recently for us and we were very pleased with his work."*
- *"He installed outside lights for our daughter's wedding reception and it made a big difference."*

Robert K. Watrous Landscape Architecture, (908)769-9866, A, 16 years in business

Using high quality low and regular voltage lighting fixtures they design night landscapes which will extend the enjoyment of a garden into the hours when one is more often home or has guests. They provide the design service and recommend contractors for installation.

- *"Bob takes pride in his work. He is inventive and creative and resourceful. He found a great company for me that makes their own lights for outdoors. I now have the most beautiful, unusual outdoor lighting. He's tops on my list!"*

DECORATIVE PAINTING

Apple Pix, (908)233-1784, UC SC , 3 years in business

Lynne Applebaum can paint in virtually any style, from intricate landscapes to cartoon figures, from trompe l'oeil to rich faux finishes. Her customers know that her job is to visualize and paint what *they* want, not what she thinks they should want. Her painting is truly versatile and matches the customer's sense of style and color. She will paint murals and also does stenciling on walls and furniture.

- *"She is wonderfully creative. A real perfectionist."*
- *"I think what is most important is that she is most interested in pleasing her clients."*

✍ ______

______

The Arbor House, (732)764-0608, A, 2 years in business

A great deal of research is done prior to the development of Mary's unique designs. She will tell the customer that 95% of all her painting, whether it be furniture, murals, accessories or stenciling, is one-of-a-kind.

- *"She does very different and unusual things. She uses different colors, not the basics. Her florals are fabulous."*
- *"She painted in the center hall of a friend's house. There were two walls—one with a classic roman bench and the other with a fern and an urn. She does neat extras and is a breath of fresh air."*

✍ ______

______

Cassidy & Company, (973)593-6826, MC, 1 year in business

Pam Cassidy describes her style of furniture painting as a sophisticated French Country look. She will customize her designs to match a fabric swatch, wallpaper or pillow. Although she has no formal artistic training, she has had many years of experience prior to going into business on her own. She says: "I have always liked color and fooling around with paint and decoupage."

- *"She did custom handpainted stools for my kitchen. She's a wonderful artist and has great ideas."*
- *"She will basically paint whatever you would like her to."*

✍ ______

______

Trish Cheek Decorative Painter, (908)232-3927, A, 5 years in business

Each piece of handpainting by Trish Cheek is a custom original. She coordinates the customer's wooden piece or wall with curtains, sofas or even a print or painting by taking part of the design and using it as the basis of the finished piece. No stencils are used.

- *"Trish is really a find. She can make a dull piece of furniture be a standout. We have used her for several projects in the house and every one was beautifully and creatively painted."*

✍ ______

Final Touch, (973)831-8562, A, 14 years in business

Anything that can be decorated with paint is tackled by Brenda Chadnick-Siclari. She provides period finishes and effects including wallpapering, faux painting, stenciling, gilding, marbling, glazing, color wash, wood graining, trompe l'oeil, aging painting, ragging and texturized stone walls. She can and will create your fantasy finish on anything.

- *"She painted an old finish in my bedroom. She's good, neat and very reliable. I think she is very talented and would definitely use her again."*

Finishing Touches, (732)321-9177, A, 8 years in business

The faux finishes done by Lois Zullo give otherwise flat walls, depth, warmth, and movement. All finishes are custom-tinted in the customer's home to coordinate with decor. Freehand florals and vine can be painted over doorways, windows, and more to give homes a special one-of-a-kind look.

- *"She faux painted my two-story center hall. I had explained to her exactly what I wanted and she did it exactly the way I wanted. Beautiful, beautiful work! A very honest businesswoman."*

The Garden Party, (908)464-5600, UC WC, 5 years in business

These are two artistic people who can help make your room very special with personalized handpainted items.

- *"They can take a wallpaper and duplicate it onto furniture. Very creative."*
- *"Especially in a child's room, she can just do very clever and wonderful finishing touches."*

Daryl Hastings, (908)730-7271, MC SC , 15 years in business

The style of Daryl Hastings' decorative painting can be best described as of a sophisticated nature giving it a timeless quality. Ordinary spaces can be transformed into extraordinary rooms. Working along with her husband, she designs, builds and finishes handpainted furniture, ranging from traditional and primitive styles to highly decorated Chinoiserie.

- *"A true artist. She has done a number of things for us. She handpainted a sissel rug to match fabric in our sunroom. She faux-painted a table and textured a table to my specifications to go in a den. She painted ducks on the table and did research before to make sure they were the ducks that I wanted. She also painted two murals in my son's room with different themes."*

Jonathan G. Hress, (973)655-1474, UC MC WC 10 years in business

Completely custom work is done by Jonathan Hress. Every piece is unique in design.

Murals, furniture, trompe l'oeil and special finishes are all specialities. He also provides a color-consulting service.

- *"Extremely artistic. He faux-painted my living room and painted a mural in one of our bathrooms. Everything was painted without a sketch—freehand. I just told him what I wanted and he did it."*
- *"He works quickly and meticulously. He is polite and clean and I was very, very pleased. He actually wrote me a beautiful letter thanking me for having him do work in my home."*

 _____

Ihnken's Creations, (607)539-3035, MC SC, 3 years in business

Since 1994 Ihnken's Creations has restored vitality to old furniture and transformed new furniture into beautiful, functional artwork. A small business with a focus on quality handwork, Ihnken's Creations offers: unique, handpainted designs on all types of furniture; work in a variety of glazes; marbleizing and other faux finishes; and custom work to match the client's decor. She enjoys transforming ordinary pieces of furniture into functional artwork.

- *"Absolutely the best! She's a sensational person, very talented. She painted a huge trousseau chest for my daughter as a shower gift and it was beautifully done beyond belief."*
- *"She showed me pictures of an entire nursery where she had painted the furniture and it was an absolute 'wow.'"*
- *"She paints and does so many wonderful things, from stationery to placemats. I recommend her very highly!"*

 _____

JPM Originals, (908)879-6728, A, 20 years in business

Daniel and Judy Mulligan will paint on any surface. Their decorative painting expertise includes murals, trompe l'oeil, glazing, marbleizing, faux wood, stenciling, venetian plaster, gilding, restoration on walls, floors, ceiling and furniture. Interestingly they not only work within this geographical area, but will travel throughout the United States.

- *"Painted an oil cloth for my kitchen 8 years ago. They do great work and I would definitely use them again. They were recommended to me by a wonderful decorator."*

 _____

Libby's Interior Painting, (908)788-4906, SC , 7 years in business

The art of stenciling has been mastered by Libby Havel. She will coordinate all stencils with the theme of the decor in the room.

- *"She did stenciling in my dining room and foyer. She's good and dependable."*
- *"She's great at offering suggestions and recommending patterns. Awfully patient. She's a sweet person. I like her a lot!"*

_____

Nirvana Furniture Creations, (973)746-0543, UC MC, 3 years in business

One-of-a-kind designs for handpainted furniture is the specialty of Nirvana. A variety of styles is available fo the customer from traditional surface treatments to whimsical pieces.

- *"Beth paints beautifully on furniture. She uses lots of color. I know she has great talent."*

Olsen Design, (908)953-9024, MC SC, 10 years in business

A home is a reflection of the people that live within. Being skilled in all forms of decorative painting Suzanne will do that special piece of furniture or wallglazing, trompe l'oeil, marbleizing, murals, woodgraining and antiquing.

- *"She is just great. She marbleized some countertops and fireplaces for me and people cannot believe it is not real marble. I have a lot of marble in my home and she matched it incredibly."*

The Painted Delphinium of Cedar Brook Farm, (908)754-3899, A, 6 years in business

The Painted Delphinium captures the splendors of nature with a wide array of distinctive and unique products and services including: custom handpainted furniture, cabinetry, floor screens, murals and floor cloths.

- *"I have never had any work done by them; however, I have seen lots of their work and it is just beautiful. So artistic. They paint to perfection on walls and furniture."*
- *"They are great girls to work with. They're imaginative and professional. They painted all the furniture in our daughter's bedroom and painted the walls in our kitchen. They do creative and very individualized painting."*

Joan Pakenham, (908)232-3901, UC, 10 years in business

Joan applies custom-designed, handpainted borders and large-cut stencils. She uses a dry-brush shading technique that achieves an advanced laying on of colors—resulting in a beautiful, multicolored and detailed look. Stencils are laser-cut for realistic and intricate patterns. They have multi overlays and come in an array of patterns with coordinated sized borders, corners and mural or trompe l'oeil effects. If the customer wants to work with a motif from a fabric or a piece from a room, Joan can custom-design a border.

- *"Joan did a sample of her stenciling on a board for me which was to be done in our bedroom. Her work is fabulous. She did a freehand stencil for me to look at which was copied after an Oriental screen in my dining room."*
- *"Her faux painting and ragging is just fabulous. She knows how light affects paint and how to deal with it in her work. Her interpretation of colors is phenomenal."*

Kimberly Petruska Designs, (610)261-4508, A, 8 years in business

This decorative painter loves to take an ordinary room and make the walls disappear—emerging as a space that has a distinctive feel and is fun to look at. She will handpaint on all surfaces and specializes in faux finishes such as sponging and ragging. She is quick to point out that these are only two of the hundreds of finishes available to recreate the beauty of marble, stone, semiprecious stones and metals. Most finishes either hide or utilize wall imperfections which makes them wonderful for older homes. Quite often she will continue a theme from fabrics or wall/floor coverings and create a mural design.

- *"She does absolutely exquisite work. We have had her marbleize the walls in our entryway and it was spectacular. We continue to receive compliments."*

Penny Pray Antiques & Accessories, (908)232-9584, UC, 12 years in business

Penny has the ability to work with the customer and present a job that is personalized in design and color. She will make up complete color boards so that the customer can see what they're getting. Stenciling on walls, floors andfurniture are done with accuracy.

- *"I am so pleased with her work. She stenciled a border of ivy around the room (which is an all-year-round sunporch). Very cleverly and naturally done. I have gotten so many compliments on her work. Penny is a lovely person."*

Marla Janes Russo, (908)889-8851, UC SC MIC, 20 years in business

Translating the customer's ideas into tangible works of art is the specialty of this painter. Without the use of stencils, she is able to draw on freehand techniques gleaned through years of portraiture and reproducing works of old masters. Her diversity is evident with matching colors and designs from the customer's wallpaper and fabrics onto furniture, walls and accessories. Animal motifs are a particular favorite. Marla says, "The brush does not rest until the customer is thrilled with the work."

- *"She paints in a very interesting way. Very creative and very talented. She painted a small table for my bathroom with a seashell on it to match the wallpaper."*
- *"In our daughter's room we have a baseball theme. She painted baseball card replications and bats on the dresser. Her portfolio is magnificent and to quote my daughter, 'She's really nice, Mom.'"*

Cyndy Saul Custom Wall Decoration, (908)233-6634, UC MC, 5 years in business

Paint with personality describes Cyndy Saul's work. She offers the customer alternatives to traditional wallpaper by handpainting walls and a variety of other services such as trompe l'oeil, stenciling, and floor painting. Custom looks can be accomplished with manipulation of wall glazes to coordinate with existing room elements.

- *"What a fantastic artist! She's professional, innovative and incredibly talented. I owned an antique shop and had gifts. We used her for various customers and she painted a dresser for one of our customers that was a delight to see."*

Ann Turnley Decorative Painting, (973)540-9767, MC SC, 8 years in business

Ann has experience with a full range of decorative treatments from faux finishes, trompe l'oeil, murals and effects, stenciling and gilding. She will paint tile as well as furniture and floor cloths. She is able to work directly with the clients to develop an idea suited to their particular space and needs.

- *"As an interior decorator, I have had the fortune to work with Ann on many occasions. She paints furniture beautifully and the customers absolutely love her work. She is excellent at trompe l'oeil and she can make surfaces look like they are inlaid wood."*
- *"I have seen her faux painting on woodwork and she can make it look like mahogany or pine."*
- *"I had the pleasure of asking Ann to create a coffee table for me from raw wood to be placed in a silent auction benefit for a school. When she finished the piece everyone on the committee wanted it. It was painted black with very intricate design in a Chinoiserie style. She is definitely a gifted artist."*

Wooden Treasures, (732)752-9634, A, 5 years in business

If you're stuck for ideas for a child's room, this talented lady will paint any character or cartoon theme from two feet to seven feet high. She specializes in folk art items and decorations and wooden lawn and outdoor decorations. Custom-made pieces are available to match existing decor or wallpaper.

- *"She is absolutely precise with color. She can copy anything from a magazine to a point beyond belief and put it on your walls."*
- *"She's creative and will work with your ideas, but will also suggest great ones on her own. She does beautiful work stenciling on furniture. She's also a fabulous person."*

Gabriella Zeltvayova, (908)769-0716, A, 3 years in business

Gabriella ia an artist/muralist who specializes in faux finishing, trompe l'oeil custom furniture finishes and gilding. She works directly with the customer or decorator to achieve the desired look.

- *"She is working in my home right now. A very accomplished artist. She has painted trompe l'oeil bookcases, faux finishes and furniture. She has done it all for me. She calls herself a 'residential artist.'"*

DRIVEWAYS

DRIVEWAYS

Edward M. Cash Paving, (908)789-6805, A, 24 years in business

With personal attention given to each job Edward Cash does all types of asphalt for driveways, car parking lots and private roads. Also included in their services are: interlocking brick pavers, Belgian block, railroad ties, retaining walls and all types of gravel.

- *"They paved our driveway one year ago. We were very pleased with their service and the job was completed with as little disruption as possible to our family. We have had no problems since."*

Colucci Paving, (732)752-1092, UC MC SC MIC, 10 years in business

Colucci is owner-operated, not just owner-supervised. They own their own equipment from small driveway pavers and rollers to highway-class machinery. Asphalt paving can be done on everything from residential driveways to parking lots and roads.

- *"This company does good quality work. They did a particularly good job directing the drainage the right way."*

Oliver A. Howarth Excavating & Paving, (908)753-7281, UC, 52 years in business

The Howarth firm excavates and paves driveways and parking lots. Workers are trained in each phase of the job. All materials used are of the highest quality and adapted to customer specification.

- *". . . work is good, clean, neat and very careful."*
- *"He has done two driveways for us. He does quality work. We've known him for 30 years and would recommend him very highly."*

Jeffrey Paving Inc., (732)549-1829, UC SC MIC WC, 41 years in business

References are proudly furnished by Jeffrey Paving. The owner oversees every job which consists of paving and concrete work for residential and commercial properties.

- *". . . did a job at the end of our long driveway. They came within days and stayed until the job was completed. We have had no problems—he did a wonderful job!"*

R. Mellusi & Sons Inc., (908)464-6676, UC MC SC, 30 years in business

Mellusi has been doing paving and construction for over 30 years. They do road construction, driveway paving, curbs and parking lots for both commercial and residential customers.

- *"The deal was to do the driveway while we were on vacation. They stayed to our schedule and got the job done. This was four years ago and we have had no problems since. Superb job!"*

_____

_____

Antonino Pafumi Contractor, (908)232-4236, UC MC SC MIC, 37 years in business

Pafumi is a family-owned-and-operated business. They take great pride in their workmanship and the quality of materials used. Specialities include the installation of asphalt driveways, parking lots and curbing. They also service the customer with excavation of waterlines and sewers and complete backhoe and loader service for any job.

- *"Pafumi put a driveway in for us two years ago. They did a great job—neat. They dug deep enough to give a nice thick layer of asphalt and installed drainage pipes so as to not cause a water problem."*
- *"They installed a sidewalk around the perimeter of my home. We are absolutely meticulous and were totally pleased with his work."*

_____

_____

William A. Parkhurst & Sons Inc., (908)233-1738, A, 80 years in business

Parkhurst is a well-known name for driveway paving. They strive to provide the customer with detailed workmanship by using quality materials.

- *". . . totally redid our driveway two years ago, which we desperately needed. They did a quality job with quality workmanship. I never let anyone work at my home when I am not there. However this was done while we were on vacation and I never worried."*
- *"They replaced our entire driveway two years ago. They were very professional, efficient and worked quickly. They protected the Belgian block borders very nicely. They have done work for us in the past and we have been always more than satisfied."*

_____

_____

Lou Porchetta Inc., (908)561-1210, A, 25 years in business

Treating every job as if it was their own home is the credo of Lou Porchetta. They do both residential and commercial paving. No job is too big or too small—they handle everything.

- *"They paved one driveway several years ago. We have had no problems since. The job was completed in the time frame that he promised. I would highly recommend him—his employees were very nice.*
- *"They did a great job. They were very careful to not ruin our landscaping. They do neat, clean work and were very attentive to the way our property sloped for drainage reasons. We would definitely use him again."*

_____

_____

Toresco & Sons, Inc., (908)756-8515, UC SC MIC WC, 72 years in business

Three generations of service has been provided by Toresco & Sons. The owner is on the job site at all times. They like to service the customer who is looking for quality workmanship for their driveway whether it be paving or installing Belgian blocks.

- *"Thorough job. They were neat and tidy—no mess and they cleaned everything.*
- *"We have a long drive—huge. They did an excellent job repaving."*

Bill Wilkins Paving & Excavating, (908)754-8663, A, 30 years in business

This firm specializes in quality paving and excavating of driveways.

- *"They put in a new driveway after many years of living with a stone driveway. They did this two years ago and we have had only a small problem with drainage which he corrected immediately. He's very nice, dependable and we feel he did a fine job. He did this while we were away."*
- *"They paved our dirveway and did some drainwork for our pond. We had subsequent problems due to the nature of our pond (with heavy rain) and he came right out and was able to correct it. He is very pleasant to work with and is reliable. I can consider him a good recommendation."*

A-1 Electric Co., Inc., (908)464-3773, UC MC SC MIC, 10 years in business

A former AT&T employee, this electrician started his own business 10 years ago. His focus is on solving the real needs of homeowners and small businesses. He places an emphasis on his technical skills and personal involvement with thecustomer.

- *"He was able to resolve an electrical problem that had been in existence for years."*
- *". . . has excellent talent—no job is too small for him such as hanging a light fixture."*

Advent Electric, Inc., (908)352-0281, A, 16 years in business

This general electrical contractor has professional technicians who are trained to provide the customer with skills to solve every electrical problem. Service calls are handled within 24 hours and emergency calls are handled promptly. All work is guaranteed.

- *"I was extremely pleased that when I had an emergency they were there within hours."*
- *"He spent a lot of time resolving our problems."*
- *"Agreeable, pleasant guy."*

William J. Allen Electrical Contractors Inc., (973)822-0955, UC MC SC, 26 years in business

Allen is an electrician that takes pride in the fact that 90 percent of his customers are repeat business. His specialties, in addition to general electrical work, include air conditioning. All work is guaranteed.

- *"Very nice person."*
- *"Methodical."*
- *"Puts all his effort into completing a job satisfactorily."*

Amptek Electrical Contractors, (973)427-6965, MC, 6 years in business

Quality of service is important to this electrical business. Customers are both commercial and residential.

- *"Did outside lighting. Had to locate various existing wires and did no damage to the property at all."*
- *"He does methodical and excellent work!"*

R.T. Brown Electrical Contracting, Inc., (732)458-6810, A, 7 years in business

An owner-operated business not limited to electrical work. Consultations with the customers continue through the duration of the job. He has 15 years experience, seven of which he has been self-employed.

- *"Came to me on a recommendation from my builder—very trustworthy in my home."*
- *"Really great guy!"*
- *". . . totally knowledgeable about all electrical problems."*

Richard V. Carney Electrical Contractors, Inc., (908)277-6961, UC MC WC, 12 years in business

Rick Carney strives to accommodate customers with honesty and integrity. Areas of expertise include interior and exterior lighting design. All types of elecrical contracting are included from relamping fixtures to alleviating serious electrical concerns.

- *"Being in the air-conditioning business for many years, I not only use Rick for all my work but recommend him to all my customers."*
- *". . . have used him for 10 years . . . dependable, punctual and neat!"*

Bernard B. Crecca Friendly Electrical Service, (908)322-7996, A, 32 years in business

Crecca's Friendly Electrical Service is a firm with 32 years of experience in residential and commercial wiring of all types. He provides prompt, efficient service with a one-year guarantee on all work performed.

- *". . . has worked in my home for 20 years."*
- *"He is a very responsive, reliable , prompt and neat person."*
- *"I consider him a friend."*

Evergreen Electric, Inc., (908)832-5454, MC SC WC, 22 years in business

This is a small company that gives personalized service to the customer. Listening to the problem and combining that with their own expertise, they devise the best solutions to accomplish the job. Having been in the trade for 35 years (22 in business for themselves), they know how to pay attention to detail.

- *"Patience is a virtue! He put up with a lot of my anxieties and handled it beautifully!"*
- *". . . very accommodating—offers wonderful suggestions."*
- *"Dependable, good work and pleasant to have in my home."*

Faraone Brothers Electrical Contractors (908)276-1666, UC, 15 years in business

The owner of this small electrical firm personally oversees every job. His goal is to build a reputation for doing quality work in a timely, courteous manner.

- *"Has installed numerous fixtures at my home which included exhaust fans, attic fans and even outside searchlights. We were more than satisfied with his work."*
- *"Decent person . . . clean and neat."*

✍ _____

Fritz Electric Company, (908)233-3748, UC SC MIC, 18 years in business

This gentleman received an electrical journeyman's license in Germany in 1962. He has been living here since 1968 and started his own company in 1979. He performs all types of electrical services—repair or maintenance.
- *"Extremely responsive. Came to our home at 10:30 p.m. for emergency problem. Solved the problem with good humor even at that hour of the night!"*
- *"When he says he's going to be there he's there. Very professional."*

✍ _____

Peter Horan Electrical Contractor, (973)538-7890, MC, 13 years in business

With 44 years experience, Peter Horan and his two sons always try to provide good quality workmanship. Mr. Horan did his electrical apprenticeship in England and transferred this knowledge to the United States. He provides not only general electrical service but also does computer and cable installation.
- *"We have used the Horans satisfactorily for many years. They have been knowledgeable and helpful in many unique situations."*
- *"Good problem solvers and extremely nice."*

✍ _____

Kennelly Electric, Inc., (908)232-4096, A, 20 years in business

Residential and commercial wiring are the noted expertise of this electrician. He has been in the business for 20 years servicing local contractors and customers.
- *"They have been our electricians since I can remember. Very dependable, totally reliable."*
- *"They are very responsive and so nice to deal with. We have had some strange electrical problems because we live in an old, old house. They know how to fix everything."*

✍ _____

Jack King Electrical Contractors, (908)561-1723, UC SC MIC WC, 30 years in business

Jack King has been a fixture in this area for many years. His motto is, "We put our very best into our work no matter how big or small the job."
- *"Came highly recommended to me and he didn't disappoint."*
- *". . . solved an intricate problem by installing lighting in my antique French curio cabinet and did it superbly. I was impressed!"*

✍ _____

Kobliska Electric, (908)889-6175, A, 13 years in business

Renovations and installation of recessed lighting are the areas of interest for this general electrician. Every attempt is made to understand the customer's needs and consciously apply it to the job.

- *"He is the most honest person I know."*
- *"I feel incredibly safe that he is doing my electrical work."*
- *"Gives good advice and doesn't try to get more work at the time."*
- *"Can fix any problem—very accommodating."*

Lake Electric Inc., (732)364-8724, A, 20 years in business

Bill Rutledge, the owner, does residential and commercial electrical installation. He prides himself on his professionalism.

- *"Installed my attic fan, which was not an easy job, on a hot day in July. Did a great job!"*
- *"Has done good quality work for many years for me and my friends."*

Litzebauer Brothers, Inc., (732)761-4141, UC MC SC MIC, 76 years in business

Over three-quarters of a century old, Litzebauer Brothers specializes in repair, alteration and modification of electrical systems.

- *"They have been wonderfully servicing our electrical needs for years."*
- *"Their scheduling will always work into my schedule."*
- *"Exceptionally neat."*

Joseph Livingstone Electrical Contractors, Inc., (908)757-0688, UC, 8 years in business

This electrician, who has been in business for eight years, specializes in electrical contracting and design. His real love is old homes and he delights in historical renovations.

- *"Joe is like an old-fashioned technician. He is a wonderful guy that has a fascination and respect for older homes. He realizes that they were built with quality and to last. We love him."*

Meininger Electric, (908)647-3564, MC SC, 12 years in business

This is a small, personal "hands-on" firm. Computerized electrical systems and conventional switches are areas of expertise. Installation of generators, service changes or any other large or small electrical problem can be done. He works closely with architects and interior designers.

58

- *"Meininger saved our lives several times. They are so responsive to emergencies and we've had those. I like the fact that they are small."*
- *"Very, very reputable and totally dependable."*

✍ _____

_____

Robert S. Minard Electrical Contractor, (201)616-6301, UC MC, 16 years in business
A one-man business that provides personal attention, this electrician provides both residential and commercial needs. Any electrical problem is no problem to this firm.
- *"A very nice guy. Great worker."*
- *"I know that I can count on him to solve problems with electricity. He is really knowledgeable and can fix anything."*

✍ _____

_____

_____

Ken Myers Electric, (908)725-6330, UC SC MIC, 22 years in business
Someone who says they never advertise but whose business is obtained solely through referrals, is a rarity. All types of electrical work are done by this electrician, including service changes, high hats, heavy lines, air-conditioning, and electric heating.
- *"Honest as the day is long."*
- *"Great guy."*

✍ _____

_____

_____

National Electric Company, (908)868-0221, UC MC SC MIC,10 years in business
This firm provides lighting design for remodeling and new construction. Every attempt is made to give professional courteous service where the customer is #1 priority.
- *"Thoroughly enjoy working with them."*
- *"Always neat, very conscientious and pleasant to deal with."*

✍ _____

_____

Niagara Electric, (908)756-1454, UC, 53 years in business
For over half a century this family-owned-and-operated firm has been providing residential wiring expertise to customers.
- *"A neighbor, good friend and my electrician for many years."*
- *"Very reliable and easy to work with."*

✍ _____

_____

George M. Paul, Inc., (732)636-9490, MIC, 33 years in business
No customer is too small or too large for George Paul. They specialize in design lighting and landscape lighting. They also install security systems.

- *"Thorough and professional . . . a true gentleman!"*

✍ ——————————————————————
——————————————————————
——————————————————————

Perfect Circuit Electric, (732)656-0499, A, 10 years in business

This firm specializes in custom electrical work. They give every customer a lifetime guarantee for all work.

- *"They completely rewired our house when we realized everything was overloading. It was a big job but they were wonderful."*

✍ ——————————————————————
——————————————————————
——————————————————————

Polyphase Electrical Contractor, (908)789-3131, A, 24 years in business

Craig Hirsch, the owner, does all the work for Polyphase. All general electrical work is included.

- *"I have used him for several jobs in my home and found him to be extremely knowledgeable and reliable."*

✍ ——————————————————————
——————————————————————
——————————————————————

R. T. Tech Electric Company Inc., (908)754-7800, A, 20 years in business

If you have an electrical problem , Richard Little of R.T. Tech can solve it. He can do service upgrades, additions, renovations, lighting design, ceiling-fan repair, heaters, cable TV, attic exhaust fans, swimming pools, furnaces, air-conditioning units and much, much more. He also provides an emergency service.

- *". . . just a really nice guy. He comes right away and is very clean and neat. He does nice work. He hung our chandeliers and did outside lighting and lanterns on the porch."*
- *"He has done all my electrical work. He came at 9P.M. one night to work on our house because I was having a party the next day. Once you find someone like this you don't want to lose him."*

✍ ——————————————————————
——————————————————————

Schoendorf Electric Inc., (908)232-1555, UC, 12 years in business

Nick Schoendorf handles "everything electrical, from plug to pole." An electrical contractor for 12 years, he does additions, renovations and new construction.

- *"Did what others couldn't do."*
- *"Good diagnostician."*
- *"When you think an electrical problem is impossible, Nick can handle it!"*

✍ ——————————————————————
——————————————————————

Schultz Brothers Electrical Contractors, (732)302-0413, A, 8 years in business

Schultz Brothers dedicate themselves to each individual job no matter how small. They do new installations, old installations, upgrades, maintenance and renovations. It is important to them to establish good work relationships with their customers and will stay on a job till completion.

- *"They installed a chandelier in my two-story center hall. I was not concerned about their breaking anything for they were extremely careful. They were quick and to the point and were very nice people to deal with. They did a wonderful job."*

R. Vandenberg Electrical Contractor, (908)968-4812, A, 12 years in business

Being a one-man firm, Bob Vandenberg provides the customer with the utmost in personalized attention. He has been in business for over a decade providing wiring of all types to both residential and commercial customers.

- *"Very responsive. Bob has the ability to solve every electrical problem, no matter how complicated."*
- *"Really nice, understated guy."*

V. M. Electric Company, (908)233-7573, A, 35 years in business

Jimmy and Vinnie Marvosa own V.M. Electric. They have enjoyed a good reputation in the community for many years. They do residential and commercial wiring and renovation work.

- *"They are extremely reliable and very prompt."*
- *"I have used them for 13 years and consider them expert electricians."*
- *". . . did an excellent job of hanging an antique lighting fixture."*

Westfield Electrical Service, (800)595-5352, UC SC MIC, 68 years in business

The Quelly family started this business in 1929 and even today all employees are members of the family. All aspects of general electrical work are handled by this small firm.

- *"Neat, prompt . . . job done well."*
- *"They've worked for me for four years doing many jobs of varying complexity and I was never disappointed!"*

ELECTRICIANS

61

ESTATE SALES

The Attic, (908)233-1954, A, 30 years in business

The Attic will conduct estate sales and has been known to do research on antiques. Their staff have a range of specialties and expertise.

- *"They are who you want to do an estate sale. I know they have great connections to be able to get the buyers."*
- *"Very reputable."*

✍ _____
_____
_____
_____

Cartouche, (908)754-7900, A, 16 years in business

John Grady will appraise, organize and conduct estate or moving sales. He will do a complete cleanout of the premises if desired. Homes are left "broom clean" for the next owner. In addition he is an appraiser of furniture and antiques.

- *"He conducted an estate sale for my parents' home. He was knowledgeable about the market for used and antique furniture. He had great contacts in order to sell things that needed to be sold. He's sincere and competent."*

✍ _____
_____
_____
_____

Helaine Fendelman & Associates, (914)725-0292, A, 25 years in business

Helaine Fendelman has a fine arts, antiques and household personal property appraisal and sales firm. She has had 25 years experience in the art and antiques field and is a certified member and president of the Appraisers Association of America. She has written several books including *Money in Your Attic: How to Turn your Furniture, Antiques, Silver and Collectibles into Cash.* Her firm will handle sales of art or antique collections or accumulations of household items at a public sale or at auction. She will conduct tag sales.

- *"What a wonderful service! Helaine is so knowledgeable. I had the pleasure of meeting her at a course taken at NYU last summer. Subsequently, her company was written up in the* New York Times.*"*
- *"She is extremely personable and knows her stuff."*

✍ _____
_____
_____
_____

M. Thompson Kravetz, (732)295-4062, A, 17 years in business

Art Kravetz specializes in 19th- and early 20th-century American art. He will do estate sales and appraising of antiques and art work.

- *"I had a friend whose business was estate sales and she was good. Before she passed away, she asked Art to take over her business because she thought that he would run it the way she had. She totally trusted him and for good reason.*
- *"He has a wonderful reputation in our area."*

✍ _____

_____

_____

_____

David Pownell Willis, (908)757-2923, A, 26 years in business
Estate and tag sales and the sale of very valuable and distinctive collections of fine and decorative are all handled by David Willis. He will make auction arrangements and only accepts high-end sales.
- *"He has a very broad understanding of antiques and collectibles . . . and valuables."*
- *"He is very well-organized and does a wonderful job."*

✍ _____

_____

_____

_____

FABRIC CLEANING

Atlantic Cleaners, (732)981-9373, UC MC SC MIC, 16 years in business

A residential service, they offer cleaning of wall-to-wall carpeting, area rugs and broadloom with a claim of expertise in Oriental rugs. Your rugs will dry within two to three hours. They will clean drapes in your home and claim they are experts in the most challenging of fabrics.

- *"Good—very thorough job. Cleaned all our wall-to-wall carpentry on the first floor and our draperies in the living room."*
- *"Trusted them to clean an antique sofa and a needlepoint chair. They were exceptionally careful and did a wonderful job."*

Bedrosian Industries, (908)464-1480, UC MC SC MIC, 73 years in business

The Bedrosian company specializes in the cleaning and restoration of Oriental rugs (handmade and machine-made), wall-to-wall-carpet, and upholstery. They will hand wash area rugs as well as restore worn area by reweaving, refringing and re-dyeing. In-home services include carpet cleaning with their state-of-the-art truck-powered steam-extraction mobile units. This system is fully self-contained, which means they supply their own water source and energy source. All soil and dirty water is recovered back into their vehicle.

- *"They have cleaned our rugs many times. They're dependable, efficient and timely. Excellent job cleaning."*
- *"The people they use to pick up and redeliver and relay the carpet were very receptive and very careful when relaying the rugs so that they were centered. There were no waves. They made sure the rugs are always completely in place before leaving."*

Better Service Carpet Cleaners Inc., (908)233-0206, A, 21 years in business

This owner-operated, truck-mounted firm has been providing personalized service for every carpet and fabric for over 20 years. They want their customers to stay with them because customer satisfaction is their strongest advertisement.

- *"I have used them for years and they are excellent. He does all his own work and he cleans both my carpets and upholstery. They are extremely responsive and will come on short notice. Thoroughly reliable."*

Carpet Wizard, (732)295-8111, UC MC SC MIC, 15 years in business

The Bane-Clene truck-mounted system is used by this company when cleaning carpets and furniture. They do no advertising and rely on word-of-mouth from satisfied customers.

- *"We used him for my wall-to-wall carpet upstairs—did a wonderful job. He was clean and neat."*
- *"He's polite and very nice—a real gentleman. The carpets look great. I have given his name out to several friends and neighbors because he has always done a great job for me."*

✍ _____
_____
_____

Certified Carpet Management Inc., (908)273-8901, A, 25 years in business
Repairing water damage, drying and restoration are the specialties of Certified along with the cleaning of carpets, upholstery and wall fabrics.
- *"Wonderful people. They truly believe the customer is first. They repaired and cleaned (on short notice) my soggy waterlogged basement rug. We originally thought we would have to have it replaced. Believe me, it looks wonderful and doesn't smell. They were truly lifesavers."*

✍ _____
_____
_____

Coit Services of Central New Jersey Inc., (908)276-2929, UC MC SC MIC, 25 years in business
Coit Services will clean your draperies, carpet and upholstery. In addition, they will also do duct cleaning.
- *"They have cleaned my draperies in our dining room and living room. They rehung neatly. Very pleasant and did a great job. I would use them again."*

✍ _____
_____
_____

Cortese Cleaning Services, (973)839-9047, UC MC, 20 years in business
Cortese uses the Von Schrader VS1 Carpet Extraction System. This applies a dirt emulsifying dry foam, brushes it thoroughly into the carpet and removes both foam and dirt immediately before it can sink back down into the carpet. This simultaneous operation is an important benefit. Because only foam is used, the carpet is ready for use in an hour or so and there is no danger of shrinkage, dry-rot or mildew. All furniture is cleaned by hand.
- *"He has been cleaning my wool rugs and upholstery for years. He works alone and is meticulous."*
- *"He's wonderful!"*

✍ _____
_____
_____

Drapemasters Cleaning of America, (908)925-8581, A, 64 years in business
Draperies must be as carefully cleaned as human skills and modern equipment can provide. Drapemasters guarantees your drapery cleaning to be perfect or 100% replacement.

They strive to provide no shrinkage, perfect pleat-folding, perfect even hems and give the fabric new life. They offer window-treatment cleaning for draperies, sheers, valences, cornices, festoons, swags and jabots, balloon shades, Roman shades, vertical blinds, miniblinds and microblinds. On-site cleaning is also available.

- *"Excellent service. They pick up and deliver. Will take down and rehang."*
- *"I have used them two or three times and a friend also uses them. They do excellent work and I recommend them to anyone. It's hard to find people that clean draperies and then rehang them."*

Gaylord Only, (908)654-4092, A, 20 years in business

Gaylord provides a professional carpet and upholstery cleaning service. They also do floor waxing. They take great pride in the quality of their work because they care and enjoy doing it.

- *"He has cleaned our carpets and furniture. He's very prompt and courteous and does a good job. He's in and out in no time."*
- *"He's very popular in our area. He did an excellent job on an area rug, and dining room, living room and bedroom carpets."*

S.K. Hamrah Carpets, (800)640-3982, UC MC SC MIC, 63 years in business

Hamrah has provided Oriental rug cleaning and repair service since 1934.

- *"We have used them on several occasions. They do a very nice job cleaning my carpets. They have also cut and bound rugs for me."*
- *"Very friendly and provide a prompt service. They are professional and did a great job cleaning our rugs. I was very satisfied."*

JR's Carpet Cleaning, (973)377-7199, A, 12 years in business

This carpet-cleaning business is dedicated to educating the consumer about carpet cleaning. They say that there are four steps to a fresh, clean, healthy carpet and make all this information available in an booklet given to all their customers. They will also do drapery cleaning.

- *"He does a fine thorough job cleaning carpets. When our basement flooded, he was there quickly on an emergency basis. He siphoned out the water, deodorized our carpets to save them from mildew and rot. Sadly he had to do this for us three to four times, but I never had to get rid of the carpets because he did such a good job."*

Lombardi Carpet & Upholstery Cleaning, (973)822-1132, UC MC SC WC, 25 years in business

This small business cares about customers and quality of work. They call back within 24 to 48 hours after a job to make sure the customer is happy with their work. The owner went to school for carpet cleaning and is always aware of new trends and problems in the carpet industry. Customers can call him at home. He tries to be very honest about any problems that may arise before, during or after cleaning.

- *"I have used them several times and they have always done a beautiful job. A very good friend, who is a decorator, recommends them to all her clients."*

Mr. Steam, (732)777-1119, MIC, 5 years in business
Mr. Steam is a family-owned-and-operated business that provides a quality service with a personal touch. They will do carpet and upholstery cleaning.

- *"A real professional. He has cleaned all my carpets and he is scheduled to come back."*
- *"I have used them for two years and they always do a fantastic job."*

P.T.K. Oriental Rug Center, (973)376-0730, A, 22 years in business
Care and repair of handwoven Oriental rugs is the area of expertise for this company. They will clean, repair and restore all kinds of Orientals—new, old and antique.

- *"We have had two of our Oriental carpets cleaned by P.T.K. They did a very good job."*
- *"They will pick up and deliver and will take the time to reinstall. Extremely nice people to deal with."*

Rug Renovating Co., Inc., (973)675-8313, A, 102 years in business
Any business that has been around for over 100 years has a lot of experience in their field. Rug Renovating does in-home cleaning of carpets and they also provide furniture (upholstered and wood) and handmade rug-cleaning services.

- *"We have used them for the cleaning of my Oriental rugs. They pick up and deliver and do a wonderful job."*
- *"They cleaned our dining room Oriental rug. They picked up and delivered and laid the carpets. They did an excellent job. They were also highly recommended as being specialists in Oriental rug cleaning."*

Service One, (973)228-1806, MC, 12 years in business
This is a small company dedicated to performing quality service. They are certified by the IIRC (Institute of Inspection, Cleaning and Restoration Certification). The owner Charles Cannistraci is certified as a Master Cleaning Technician—one of only two in the state of New Jersey. They believe in an old-fashioned work ethic and do very little advertising, obtaining most work from customer recommendations.

- *"He cleans our upholstery and rugs. At one point there was a stain on a rug that three other companies could not get out but he did."*

- *"He was able to get cat vomit off a chair. My husband is a pediatrician and he uses him in the office. He gets all kinds of formula stains out of waiting-room chairs and the carpet."*
- *"We have friends who own a senior-citizens home and they use him all the time. He is fantastic. Unbelievable."*

✎ _____
_____
_____

Stempler's Drapery, (973)923-0919, A, 87 years in business

Stempler's was established in 1910 to service the residential community with professional drapery cleaning and alterations. Their patented Adjust-A-Drape system guarantees the length of the draperies will not be altered. Their full service includes removal, cleaning and reinstallation.

- *"They do a wonderful job of drapery cleaning. They take down the treatments and will rehang. To rehang can be difficult with certain draperies but they know what they are doing. I highly recommend them."*

✎ _____
_____
_____

Wells Rug Service, (973)539-3800, MC SC, 76 years in business

Wells will wash rugs by hand and provide Oriental rug cleaning.

- *"Best name in town for Oriental carpet cleaning. Whenever my rugs need to be cleaned, I always use Wells. They do a great job and have a wonderful reputation."*

✎ _____
_____
_____

FABRIC CLEANING

FENCING

Artistic Fence Company, (800)Fence16, UC MC, 14 years in business
All types of residential fences from wood, PVC to aluminum and chain-link are installed by this company. This is an owner-operated business.
- *"They installed a fence in our backyard eight years ago. They did exactly what we wanted and were very professional."*
- *"We had no problems with these people. Whenever I want another fence I would not hesitate to call them."*

Eagle Fence and Supply Inc., (973)526-5775, A, 30 years in business
Two generations of family make up this fencing business. Dealing with people is an important part of their daily work. They have a diversified inventory with everything from pool, yard and pasture fences but one can also purchase top soil, mulch, landscape ties, sheds, decks, kennels, swing sets and flagpoles.
- *"This company installed a fence for us in 1995. They were very professional and we have had no problems."*

Rudl Fencing & Decking, (800)599-RUDL, A, 54 years in business
Today, when the average person has to work hard to provide a comfortable, attractive place to live and raise a family, value is very important. Rudl Fencing makes a conscious effort to provide affordable fencing alternatives. Their fences run the gamut from wood, chain-link and PVC to ornamental iron and aluminum. They have more than 10,000 square feet of indoor and outdoor displays to help the customer choose the right materials. Also available are more than 100 different finials and spindles which provide unlimited fence design possibilities.
- *"I am a contractor and builder and I just used them on a recent project. The materials they use are excellent. If you want beautiful country fencing I can surely recommend them."*

Walpole Woodworkers, (973)539-3555, A, 64 years in business
Walpole manufactures quality fence, furniture and small buildings. All kinds of fencing, including cedar and anchor chain-link, are designed and installed. All wood is milled in the company's mills in Maine to insure quality control.
- *"I cannot say enough good things about them. We are from the Boston area and they are truly a tradition in that part of the country. I can't tell you how thrilled I was to learn they are now in New Jersey."*

- *"They are highly dependable, provide quality workmanship and have a well-established business."*
- *"Their fences are truly classic and there is a wonderful design staff available to help you decide what kind of fence best suits your property and what the configuration should be. I hope as a result of this book they get lots and lots of business."*

FLOORING & FLOOR COVERING

Barry Biederman Flooring, (908)788-9418, A, 20 years in business
Barry Biederman is a shop-at-home flooring business. He installs linoleum sheet vinyl and vinyl tile. All the work is done personally by this owner-operator.
- *"He installed a vinyl floor in our kitchen and did a really nice job. He's conscientious, punctual and neat and a great guy. I would definitely use him again."*

Contemporary Flooring, (908)322-7979, A, 19 years in business
This company can restore your old floor or provide you with a wide selection of new floor coverings from antique woods to state-of-the-art laser-cut inlays. Theytake pride in choosing only the best mills for their woods and only the best environmentally safe Swedish acrylic finishes that are proven to be more durable than oil-base urethane. They will also provide the customer with the proper cleaning kits, and help maintain floors. Advice on floor-covering needs—whether a laminate, solid or a floating floor—is provided.
- *"We have an old home and they did 'cosmetic' touching to my master bedroom suite. I just could not go through having the floors completely done over and what they did really satisfied us. They are wonderful to work with."*
- *"They come on time and have great customer follow-up care."*

Expert Floors, (973)378-8858, UC MC WC, 20 years in business
European craftsmanship is employed when this company installs and refinishes hardwood floors.
- *"Our decorator recommended them and we found them to be reliable. They do a very good job with staining and refinishing."*

Floor Coverings International, (908)668-1184, A, 3 years in business
FCI is a franchised shop-at-home business, stressing a level of service that most stores can't provide. They keep up-to-date with the latest fashion styles and colors, bringing samples into the customers' home. They do their own measuring, layout, and installation and provide a written labor warranty in addition to the manufacturer's warranties. Products include: carpet, area rugs, linoleum, tile, and imported wood laminates.
- *"Besides being a really nice man to deal with, he has a great business."*
- *"My feeling is why go to a store when he can come to you with the latest in carpets and you can see all the samples in the room with your sofa chairs and furnishings."*
- *"He's wonderful and what a great service!"*

Gruber Hardwood Floors, (908)381-7909, A, 30 years in business

Joe Gruber gives individual attention to his customers. He provides a range of wood-floor services including: installation, sanding, finishing, staining, borders and pickling.

- *"He stained and refinished our floors. He also did a custom stain for us that is wonderful. He is very accommodating and meticulous."*

 _____

Thomas J. Hamill Flooring Contractor, (732)752-1241, A, 45 years in business

A thorough explanation of procedures and products is provided for the customer by Tom Hamill. He will do floor sanding, staining, refinishing of interiors and also provides a service for decks.

- *"He sanded and refinished our floors. We dreaded the job but believe it or not he actually made it a semipleasurable experience. He's a very nice guy and extremely knowledgeable."*

 _____

Harty Brothers Carpet & Vinyl Inc., (908)753-0044, A, 65 years in business

This third-generation business specializes in all types of flooring.

- *"We have used them for 10 years. They have installed carpeting and vinyl and tile floors. We have always been very satisfied."*
- *"They are pleasant, nice, friendly people. They always have had good installers. They provide a prompt, courteous service."*

 _____

Irvington Linoleum & Carpet, (908)494-1976, A, 38 years in business

The right combination of service and quality installation is the goal of this company. Their main area of expertise lies with new construction and the installation of carpet, linoleum, prefinished wood and vinyl tile.

- *"Twenty-five years of personal experience with Irvington Linoleum and we find that they have been consistent with quality service and friendly accommodating customer relations. No other carpet business in the area comes close to their professional expertise as well as a wide variety of residential and commercial carpets. Their accommodating staff, convenient location and beautiful merchandise makes this anyone's best choice."*

 _____

King Wood Floors, (908)654-1165, A, 9 years in business

John and Ed together have 40 years of experience with floors. They will sand, refinish, and provide custom colors and staining. They try to leave every job as if they were living there themselves.

- *"These guys are wonderful! They do a great job sanding and refinishing floors. Our old hardwood floors look beautiful and we love the way they stained our kitchen floor. Our neighbors have used them for installing a hallway floor and they were thrilled too."*

Jim McCormick Flooring Inc., (908)454-3812, A, 49 years in business

McCormick's crew provides a service for all aspects of wood flooring including total remodeling and kitchen expansions. They pride themselves on working out job details and being very flexible with scheduling.

- *"They are thorough and quick. They put down a new hardwood floor in our kitchen. When it came to the color of the stain, I was really fussy and he was exceptionally patient with me until we came up with the perfect color."*

Rees Powell Custom Floors, Inc., (908)889-7944, A, 77 years in business

The first sanding machine in the state of New Jersey was owned by the grandfather who established this business in 1920. They do laying, sanding and finishing.

- *"What a wonderful job they did refinishing floor for me. We had wall-to-wall carpeting for approximately 30 years. When it was taken up the floors were in very bad condition. After he was done they were beautiful with minimal mess."*
- *"He has done the floors in all the homes I have owned. We are always happy with his work. Floor refinishing can be messy, but he definitely keeps it at a minimum. My feeling is that a beautiful room begins with a beautiful floor and Rees Powell can achieve that. "*

Rossi & Company Inc., (973)672-6639, MC, 51 years in business

Rossi will give an abundance of free advice to customers from basic planning stages through finishing applications. After completing preliminaries, they will troubleshoot and be of help when problems or unforeseen difficulties occur.

- *"They are very dependable. Very good workers. He will never let you down. I have used him for years."*
- *"He even came down to our summer home to install floors. He lets you know exactly how long it will take to do a job and order materials. He does a really great job."*

Ted Stanek, (732)681-7796, A, 60 years in business

Having been in business for 60 years, Ted Stanek wants his customers to be pleased with his work for he values repeat business. He will sand, refinish, mix colors and stain hardwood floors.

- *"He did a wonderful job on our floors. He never left the job and stayed from start to finish. He's conscientious and efficient."*

- *"I found them to be prompt, reliable and honest. I would give him my keys without hesitation."*

✍ _____

_____

The Square Yard Inc., (908)277-4580, UC MC SC WC, 24 years in business

All aspects of flooring are done by the Square Yard. These include fine-wood flooring and refinishing, wood stripping, random plank, parquet, and custom borders.

- *"Truly competent and honest. They installed our flooring and did a great job. We never had a problem since."*

✍ _____

_____

Tooker's Carpet Service, (908)486-3087, A, 20 years in business

Mr. Tooker will take his experience in the carpet trade right to your doorstep. He has a shop-at-home service and a great supply of carpeting in his truck. He is ready to install when you are.

- *"He makes carpet shopping easy. He has an enormous selection on his truck and will bring it to your home."*
- *"He is easy to work with and very nice."*

✍ _____

_____

Viking Wood Floors, (973)887-1776, UC MC SC, 44 years in business

Viking is a small business that strives to cater to the homeowner's choice in color and design. This business was started in 1953 by Turner Litland who came from Norway. His son Bob now runs the business. His employees have on average seven years of experience each. Viking will do custom installations and borders, floor refinishing in designer tones. They pride themselves on using new, high-tech methods of floor finishing.

- *"These are very conscientious workers . They are nice guys to have around and they are very aware of environmental hazards of some of the chemicals used in the finishes and how to minimize them. In fact, we have allergic kids in the house, so we had to switch from one type of floor to another."*
- *"One thing I really, really liked was that they were very quick and efficient. And you know how important that is when you have furniture all over the house."*

✍ _____

_____

FLORAL DESIGNERS

Boxwood Designs, (908)604-8840, UC MC SC, 6 years in business

Boxwood Designs offers clients a full-custom floral interior-design service. Maureen Enderlin tries to interpret the feelings, mood and colors the client wants for their homes in her flower arrangements. She will also design wreaths and topiaries.

- *"I have a number of her floral pieces in my home. She is a very creative floral designer, especially in silks. I know her pieces have been photographed in* House and Garden.*"*
- *"Her work is superior and very creative. She does phenomenal hats and beautiful interior-design work."*

The Cutting Garden, (973)822-3572, UC MC, 6 years in business

This floral designer likes to have a personal consultation in the customer's home or location of special occasion. She does arrangements for parties, business functions and weddings both large and small.

- *"Ellen is not your everyday florist. Her creations are innovative and imaginative. She uses a lot of flowers that she grows in her own backyard, so they are really fresh. She has always been responsive to my requests and concerns."*

Richard Edgcomb Designs, (908)534-1100, MC SC WC, 10 years in business

Richard Edgcomb is a full-service floral shop which adheres to a simple design philosophy: "Challenge the mediocre with the unexpected." Drawing on the seasonal best from the N.Y. market, Holland growers, local plantings and wildflowers, Edgcomb produces cutting-edge work. Daily orders are usually placed in clear-glass vases and styled in the tradition of English gardens. They have a supply of twig, grapevine, and wicker baskets for arrangements plus one-of-a-kind antique cups and saucers, old watering cans, silver urns and glassware. If fresh flowers aren't appropriate they specialize in creating freeze and air-dried arrangements of all shapes and sizes.

- *"Very creative and artistic. They do beautiful arrangements."*
- *"He's a nice guy. I had the pleasure of working with Edgcomb Designs for a benefit and their work is fabulous. There were many positive comments from the attendees. He is tops on my list!"*

The Emerald Garden, (973)564-9510, A, 5 years in business

The floral designers of Emerald Garden will provide arrangements for weddings, parties, plantings and all floral needs.

- *"Oh, he's fabulous. He did a magnificent job for our daughter's wedding. He's very innovative and fun to work with. I never had him do anything for me that I was unhappy with."*

75

- *"He's fun to work with, has lots of talent and most of all is dependable."*

The Enchanted Garden, (908)709-1010, UC, 3 years in business

A fantasy wedding, party or special will come alive with a unique floral arrangement from Enchanted Garden. Whether it be a garden-style fresh arrangement, or custom silk- or dry-arrangement, they will personally see to it that the homeowner is pleased with the end result.

- *"They are very creative and artistic. Very dependable. They will do anything from a small hostess gift to creating arrangements for a large party at home."*
- *"She has a very unique style. She uses natural wildflower designs and does not just stay with traditional designs. I just have very good things to say about Enchanted Garden."*

Ferguson & McQuillan, (908)791-1224, A, 3 years in business

The finest dried and natural materials are used in arrangements by Ferguson & McQuillan. The look is as beautiful as fresh flowers with the added advantage of lasting for a lifetime. Containers used by these designers are especially creative and may be ceramic, terra-cotta, Oriental copper or wicker or something belonging to the customer. Custom designs are created for the home and business decor and they are also available to decorate for the holidays.

- *"I have had a wall hanging by Ferguson & McQuillan made for my kitchen. The colors are perfect. They did a beautiful job."*
- *"They made an absolutely terrific artichoke wreath for my kitchen. I love it."*
- *"They make very creative—even artistic—arrangements. They can customize to the client's needs. Once a year the client has the option of viewing work by them in their place of work. It's a wonderful way to get ideas!"*

Beverlee Fisher Designs, (973)467-4477, A, 15 years in business

From whimsical antique chandeliers to beautiful freeze-dried and natural-flower arrangements, Beverlee Fisher can transform the ordinary into a lovely garden. Her "Signature Old World"–style arrangements contain beautiful flowers, rich ribbons, marble and glass fruits, hydrangeas, pepperberries, beaded flowers, pearls and more. Any type of design can be created from Country French to traditional or contemporary. An interesting sideline is Beverlee's Fake Cakes. These are made from freeze-dried flower petals and blossoms.

- *"Beverlee is very, very creative. If you want something different and unique she is the one to do it. She can do anything from funky to conservative arrangements and do it well. I have several of her arrangements in my house and have been so satisfied with them. I also love to visit her shop."*

Flowers . . . Naturally, (908)233-0905, A, 8 years in business

The client's individual needs and desires are attended to by the personalized service offered by Kay Cross. Her flowers are carefully hand-selected and purchased for each specific occasion. She offers choices of fresh, silk or dried arrangements and loves an open airy look with a European feel. Kay will make arrangements for any special occasion and provides a holiday decorating service.

- *"She's great! Always uses wonderful, fresh flowers."*
- *"She did a private New Year's Eve party for us and the centerpieces were fabulous. She has done four separate occasions for me and they were all fabulous."*

Jardiniere, (973)763-2830, A, 13 years in business

A distinctive, high-style floral design business, Jardiniere will decorate your home for special parties, holidays and "just because." In addition to flowers, they will also work with plants to enhance areas within the home. They will also make suggestions on linens and a host of other items to add that very special touch.

- *"Wonderful to work with. Very professional and designs beautifully."*

L'Memories, (908)754-1888, MC SC MIC, 15 years in business

L'Memories will offer you in-home decorating services with fresh or silk plants and flowers. For that special party or event they can supply you with linens, floral decoration and more.

- *"I actually used them to cater a party for 60 people in my home. They did a professional, beautiful job. They also offer a flower-decorating service and he did all the arrangements."*

A New Leaf, (973)763-5055, UC MC WC, 15 years in business

From parties and weddings to Inaugural Balls, this floral designer has created unusual arrangements. She specializes in Greenplant interiorscape and provides plants and containers. On the exterior—patios and decks—she will arrange container gardens.

- *"She is superb! She does spectacular work. She works very nicely with us and listens to everything carefully."*
- *"She has a real rapport with her customers."*

The New Leaf Florist, (800)752-9453, A, 4 years in business

Natural and unusual botanicals are incorporated in all the arrangements made by these

FLORAL DESIGNERS

77

talented florists. They provide floral arrangements and designs for parties (both corporate and personal), weddings, Christmas decorations, floral window treatments, and botanical decorating of decks and patios.

- *"Does really sharp stuff."*
- *"She's into nature and baskets. She works hard at making everything special."*

Pamela Newell Designs, (908)654-3614, UC MC SC WC, 10 years in business

Pamela gives individual attention to each project. Her original designs have an English garden flair. As a full floral-decorating service, she will personally create lovely arrangements and designs for the holidays, weddings or parties at home using custom silk, dried or fresh flowers. As a special plus, she will design and install a perennial garden.

- *"She did our interior Christmas decorations with beautiful ribbons and pinecones. The mantel pieces were just beautiful."*
- *"She made wreaths for our doors. She's good with custom work and has style and uses color well."*
- *"A friend of mine used Pam to decorate her home for a Christmas wedding. It was breathtaking!"*

Plants Plus Andi, (800)554-2634, A, 9 years in business

Andi offers a wide range of services including custom arrangements and expert wedding and party planning. Need advice on creating a perennial garden or planting containers and window boxes? They will come to your home or office and plant it for you. They also have a wide variety of unique plants and great containers.

- *"I think she has nothing but the best. She has top quality flowers, beautiful roses— has orchids all-year-round. She does wonderful arrangements for special events."*
- *"She has beautiful annuals, perennials and herbs. One thing that I love about Andi is she will make special efforts to get what you want."*

Potpourri, (908)277-3186, A, 14 years in business

The emphasis is on fresh floral designs for Betty Fisher. She considers herself a florist/event planner and will consult with her customers for functions ranging from weddings to private parties.

- *"Betty did all the flowers for my daughter's wedding, which were absolutely magnificent. She decorated my home with the most beautiful flowers and also did very unusual fresh-flower arrangements for my back and front door."*
- *"I cannot tell you how many compliments we got from people who saw the arrangements."*
- *"She is absolutely lovely to work with and she has my highest recommendations."*

Jerry Rose Inc., (973)762-1085, A, 15 years in business

Jerry Rose provides a designer who can visit the client's home and present a proposal to accessorize the home with blooming and green plants, silk or dried arrangements. They recommend and provide interesting and unique containers for the interior as well as exterior. Entertaining in your home? They can design flower arrangements and have a party-planning service that extends to linen rental and entertainment. During the holiday they provide a home-decorating service.

- *"They do fabulous work. They're very artistic and dependable. Nice to work with and just do beautiful, beautiful work."*

Scarlet Begonias, (908)654-9735, A, 3 years in business

Having chosen a beautiful name for her business, this floral arranger sets the tone for everything she does. She provides a customized service for all occasions whether it be corporate or private gatherings.

- *"Samantha is so wonderful and very personable. She knows her customers well—their likes and dislikes. She's very creative."*
- *"She made arrangements at Christmas for our outside windowsills and our home looked lovely. Her flowers are extremely fresh."*
- *"She has made some very unusual window arrangements for my kitchen with branches and hydrangeas. At Christmas they put beautiful fresh wreaths with gorgeous ribbons on all my windows and decorated our porches."*

FURNITURE REPAIR

A Touch of the Past, (732)988-1829, UC MIC, 14 years in business

Antique furniture is a passion for Gerry Quatro. He specializes in repairing antiques and refinishing furniture from 2 to 200 years old.

- *"He repaired a Tiffany clock case for me. He repaired the marquetry on the clock. He took a lot of time and did a beautiful job."*
- *"A small piece of veneer was missing from a table of ours and he was able to replace it beautifully. He also repaired a leg on a tripod table. He does excellent work!"*

Chem-Clean Furniture Restoration, (908)322-4433, A, 25 years in business

This is a well-known furniture restoration company that specializes in stripping and metal cleaning, cabinet refinishing and repairs. They use a specially patented solvent to clean and strip furniture which avoids damaging the furniture.

- *"I feel they have the best equipment to strip paint and refinish. They stripped and painted my cabinet doors in the kitchen and they have stripped and refinished and repaired pieces of furniture for me. We have used them often and will use them again."*

Fine Woodfinishes, (973)285-5128, A, 17 years in business

Michael Sullivan's knowledge is based on 17 years of experience in antique restoration and conservation. His experiences have included restoration and conservation for Christie's and Sotheby's as well as MacCulloch Hall and the Morris Museum. His specialty is hand-rubbed finish which entails a 20-step process which enhances the natural beauty of fine wood.

- *"He repaired and restored two very old valuable tables of mine. He's an excellent craftsman and he knows how to work with old pieces."*
- *"He's prompt and you can trust him with your best furniture."*

Chod Lang, (908)534-4322, A, 12 years in business

Chod will repair furniture in your home by appointment and it is usually done the same day. He is a "one-man band" and feels great responsibility for the customer's satisfaction. He also designs and manufactures furniture and has a reputation of being sensitive to the character of the house and the client. All design work is done on the computer and he makes every effort to communicate graphically about what the final product will look like.

- *"Chod is wonderful! I found out about him through an antique dealer who highly recommended him for antique furniture repair. I had an enormous piece of furniture that couldn't be removed from the space in my home and Chod came to my home and worked on the piece in the room in my house. He also did some minor* repairs to two of my antique pieces and repaired a dining-room table for a friend. She was exceptionally happy."

- "He can show you a portfolio of all the work he has done and you will be amazed. Although he has only done repair work for me, I would definitely consider using him for construction of a new piece."

_____

_____

Loud's Strip Joint, (732)752-4040, A, 18 years in business

Mr. Loud has a complete furniture-repair business which includes stripping, and refinishing both woods and metals. Because he considers his craft an art form, he has developed an expertise and a love of repair of antique furniture.

- "He's wonderful. I do my own refinishing, however I have used him for stripping all our outside railings and many pieces of furniture. He's very dependable. We've used him for years."
- "A great guy. He really knows his business. He redid all the doors in my upstairs hall. We have an old home and he was extremely careful. I purchased two old twin beds for my sons' room and he stripped and refinished them exactly the way I wanted."

_____

_____

Maxwell's Furniture Restoration, (908)232-0226, UM MC, 103 years in business

Maxwell's has been in business for over 100 years providing their customers with the very best in craftsmanship and design. They operate under Old-World standards using methods handed down through four generations of master furniture craftsmen. They provide repair, refinishing and upholstery of any type or style of furniture including antique, period and contemporary.

- "They have refinished several old pieces for me. They do beautiful work. What I like in particular is that they are not refinished to a point where the antiques now look new—they are just finished to perfection."
- "I have used Don Maxwell for many years, as many people I know also use him. He does great work. He took an antique high chair that was literally in a hundred pieces and put it all back together, refinished it and it looks beautiful. They have been in business for years and have a great reputation."

_____

_____

Palamaro Furniture Touch-ups, (201)261-5495, A, 26 years in business

All phases of finishing, touch-up and even faux finishing is offered by this firm. In addition to residences work is done for restaurants, offices, banks, warehouses and movers.

- "I had purchased beautiful lacquered furniture in New York. One of the chairs was damaged. They recommended Palamaro to me. He completely fixed this chair so as no one could tell. Outstanding job!"
- "He has done repairs for me and he's a perfectionist."

- *"I don't know if he remembers me but he made such an impact on me, I will always call him when needed. I am neurotic and need all work done in my home to perfection. He's the guy for me. A+"*

The Restore, (908)647-0613, A, 26 years in business

Carl Sundberg specializes in complete furniture restoration, both antique and contemporary. He has done inlay and veneer repairs, carving, duplicating missing parts, carousel-horse restoration, woodcarving and fold-art restoration.

- *"Carl is a skilled craftsman intensely committed to quality and restoration of furniture. For me, he had satisfactorily restored several pieces of antique furniture damaged by fire."*

George Stummer, (908)232-7978, A, 90 years in business

Furniture restoration of all types is a passion of George Stummer, a small family-owned-and-operated business. They repair furniture damaged in moving and have developed a reputation for French polishing.

- *"He worked on several pieces of furniture for me. He was able to fix up scratches so that I was able to avoid having the entire piece or pieces refinished. Excellent job!"*

GENERAL CONTRACTORS

A & J Renovation, (908)754-8918, A, 12 years in business

If you asked A & J what they felt was distinctive about their business, they would answer with a long list—Restoration services, custom moldings, flooring and landscape design. They provide period-correct construction including columns, brackets, railings and other details.

- *"This is a very accomplished renovation firm. They have restored several small rooms in my house. When I say restore, I mean gut and rebuild. They started out by sitting down with us and determining exactly what we wanted to do. They are very knowledgeable, creative and easy to work with."*

BBJ Inc., (908)356-1512, A, 15 years in business

BBJ is a full-service remodeling firm with considerable experience in all phases of construction. In May of 1987 they were named one of the top fifty remodelers in the nation. Design guidance and product selection expertise assures the homeowner that the project will be within budget.

- *"They installed a new kitchen. They did everything possible to retain the integrity of my older home's architecture."*
- *"The addition to our house looks like it's always been there even though it's new, updated and functional."*

Bolcar Construction Co., (973)808-2833, UC MC, 7 years in business

Unlike most builders, Bolcar Construction takes on only a limited number of customers each year in order to provide a very personalized service. They provide the ultimate in flexibility by rendering design sketches by using Computer Aided Design which enables the customer to make changes before construction begins. Each phase of the building process is handled by the owner and special attention is given to custom lighting, space enhancements, comfort, function, ambiance and styling.

- *"They installed a new kitchen for us. We love it and have not had to have them back for minor adjustments."*
- *". . . completely re-did our master bathroom, including two skylights. We have never had a leaking problem like so many people we know have had."*
- *"This company installed a bay window which is very tight. They do quality workmanship and I would use him again."*

R.T. Brown Builders, (732)458-2811, A, 7 years in business

Brown is a general contractor that will work on all types of building projects, including new construction and renovations. The owner oversees all jobs thereby providing personalized, quality service.

- *"He's very good . . . honest and fair."*
- *"He installed a fountain for us—did a beautiful job."*

 _____

_____

Davidson Construction Inc., (908)233-3246, UC, 12 years in business

Peter Davidson's goal is to achieve an excellent relationship with both customers and licensed subcontractors. His specialities include building additions, alterations and kitchens.

- *". . . did major renovations on our house. The family room, great room, kitchen, deck, bathroom, new siding and windows. He is dependable, thorough, very professional, detailed and task-oriented. He's a joy to work with."*

 _____

_____

Defiore & Corbett Contractors, (908)233-6029, UC, 36 years in business

This business is a personalized custom home-contracting service. To achieve their goals, they use high-quality materials combined with excellent craftsmanship.

- *"I used them as an engineer when I purchased my home—very informative and very thorough."*
- *"Nicest people to deal with . . . top quality."*
- *"I cannot say enough good things . . . they are the best!"*

 _____

_____

Dowcon Inc., (908)232-7171, A, 12 years in business

Dowcon Inc. considers themselves a high-end custom homebuilder, remodeler and designer. Paying extreme attention to detail, they do both designing and building.

- *"They do quality work. Their trim work is perfect with the proper angles. They have an eye for design and style."*

_____

_____

Duffy's Construction, (908)665-9068, UC MC SC, 9 years in business

This construction firm is owner-operated with in-house carpenters specializing in high-end residential construction. They can work closely with the customer's architect. Main focus is on renovations of historical homes, additions, new construction, custom cabinetry, wine cellars, and construction management.

- *"They're always on time. He's an honest, great guy who knows what he's doing."*
- *"He always returns phone calls and most of all . . . he listens!"*
- *"He is a diamond in disguise. He's young, plain-spoken but a fine craftsman whose life's joy is to create gracious living space. He has an uncanny sense of the drama of space, color and size and knows his building products. Brian works synergistically with the architect and most importantly he is ruthlessly honest. All of this in a truly enjoyable human being!"*

 _____

_____

GENERAL CONTRACTORS

Phil Episcapo & Sons Home Improvement, (908)665-8673, UC MC, 14 years in business
This home-improvement company specializes in carpentry, remodeling and plaster work. They make an effort to keep business simple so as not to overextend themselves and have the quality of their work suffer. Every job is a top priority until it is completed—small or large. They will also tackle additions, kitchens and bathrooms.

- *"He's wonderful! He has done so many things in my home—plastering, carpentry and rebuilt doors. I got his name from a friend who felt the same way about him. My husband had a heart attack and was unable to do anything around the home and I gave David an extensive list which he finished in one week."*
- *"We have an old home and our screen door was the original. It needed to be replaced. The cost of a new door was too high and he said 'Let me take care of it.' He reconstructed it like new. He's an absolute treasure."*

Thomas Giannini Inc., (908)647-5971, UC MC SC, 15 years in business
Thomas Giannini is a general contractor who truly cares about quality and workmanship when constructing new homes, additions and renovations. He is proud of his work and his many satisfied customers.

- *"He put on a great room for us. We found him to be incredibly reliable, honest and forthright. He stands behind his work and follows through."*
- *"Tom was there as scheduled and stayed on the job. We could not be happier with the job he did. Whenever we are relaxing in 'his' room we realize how wonderful a job he did!"*

David D. Hengerer, (908)359-1877, A, 11 years in business
This firm manages projects from the architectural design through the completion of the building. Areas of expertise include renovation and restoration, additions, large and small remodeling projects such as kitchens, baths, and basements. Their goal is to make sure that every telephone call and inquiry is answered, because people deserve to have a response to their phone calls.

- *"They did our master bedroom and bathroom renovation . . . put in a kitchen and family room addition to our home. He is hardworking and personable and always there when he said he would. In the end he did a beautiful job."*

R. F. Hennessy Construction Inc., (908)526-3931, UC MC SC MIC, 10 years in business
A contractor who only works on one job at a time, Hennessy specializes in home improvements, carpentry, additions, renovations and enclosures. He will tackle anything and what he can't do—such as electrical, plumbing and excavating—he will subcontract.

- *". . . very nice guy. He took a panel down in the den and put up dry walls."*
- *"He did special moldings. Basically whatever we wanted done, he did."*

Hillside Construction Co. Inc., (732)549-8888, MIC, 20 years in business

A small, highly skilled staff of "hands-on" builders and carpenters is the best way to describe Hillside Construction. They will tackle anything from small jobs and additions to large single family homes.

- *"I use them for everything I possibly can. They covered a patio porch which is very elaborate and we just love the job they did."*
- *"They are now redoing my entire basement—worked well with my architect."*

_____

Anthony James Construction Inc., (908)233-2225, UC, 11 years in business

Anthony James has been lauded as one of America's best builders and remodelers by *Better Homes & Gardens* magazine for the years 1996-97. In addition, he was recognized as one of the 50 top remodelers in America by *Hanly Wood Remodeling* magazine. They specialize in residential additions and major renovations and are experts at maintaining the architectural integrity and design of a project.

- *"He did our family room addition. Everything is planned in a very organized fashion. Excellent work!"*
- *"His workers were all enjoyable to have in the house. They all had positive attitudes."*

_____
_____

JMC Development Inc., (973)386-0707, UC MC SC, 20 years in business

JMC is a full-service contracting business. If you want your basement remodeled, a new kitchen, a spacious family room or a clean and comfy bathroom, they can help you accomplish this.

- *". . . totally refinished our basement including adding a bathroom. They also enclosed an already existing porch and made it into an all-year-round sunporch. His work has stood the test of time."*
- *"He's a pleasant individual and he does good work."*

_____
_____

JMK Builders, (908)730-8050, A, 14 years in business

This is a "hands-on" contracting firm specializing in building additions. They have built everything from family rooms to bathrooms and decks. They pride themselves on making new construction look like it has been an original part of the house.

- *"Very creative people. They took a very small space and made it into a great living area."*
- *"They do quality work."*

_____
_____
_____

John A. LaMaita, Inc., (908)665-1338, A, 17 years in business

This general contractor performs a wide spectrum of services for his clients. Projects include custom additions, renovations, interior millwork, kitchens and bathrooms, library cabinets and built-in bookcases.

- *"He is very dependable and precise. He completed the work within a reasonable amount of time. If anything need to be changed he was extremely agreeable. We were very satisfied with his work."*

Maverick Builders, Inc., (201)938-0600, A, 10 years in business
Maverick only handles a limited number of projects which makes it easier to maintain quality and performance. They only accept premium quality projects which must be over $500,000.

- *"We have done four projects with them. They consistently produced great quality work and demonstrated project management."*
- *"They have met or beat our projected completion dates."*

MD Homes & Co. Inc., (908)317-0677, UC MC SC WC, 18 years in business
Whatever your needs MD Homes can satisfy you for they are both an architectural and construction firm. Therefore the client experiences a stress-free project by dealing only with one company.

- *"... did our kitchen and family room. He's a really nice guy ... a good friend. He's great to work with. I also have friends who have used him and they're very happy with his work."*

New Jersey Hardwoods, Inc., (908)754-0990, A, 16 years in business
With a reputation for quality and design, New Jersey Hardwoods, Inc. has supplied custom- home builders and homeowners with fine architectural millwork. From custom entertainment units, traditional libraries, and fireplace mantels to elegant door-entry units this firm tries to meet all the client's needs.

- *"They did an archway in our home with 40-foot pillars. They also manufactured library bookcases and put in wainscotting. They stayed with this difficult job to completion and did excellent work."*
- *"I have very high standards and am a perfectionist and they satisfied all my whims."*

P.M. Construction Corp., (973)736-7006, MC, 20 years in business
With professional and prompt service, this general contractor provides a variety of services to his customers.

- *"He responds quickly to my phone calls. Very dependable."*

GENERAL CONTRACTORS

GENERAL CONTRACTORS

- *"He was recommended to me by a friend who was also happy with him. He's very talented."*

✍ _____

_____

RHI Construction Inc., (973)605-8954, MC, 10 years in business

This firm provides quality custom craftsmanship with special attention to clients' needs. Their projects are completed in a timely manner without sacrificing attention to detail. To best describe them, they are general contractors for additions, restoration, custom carpentry and remodeling. The owner Reinhard Hilkenbach is a German craftsman.

- *"He is very good with structural work. We have an old home and when we purchased it it needed lots of work. He has done an enormous amount of projects for us. He replaced our front porch which is huge."*
- *"He is trustworthy and has excellent subcontractors. I was working when most of this was going on and did not feel at all ill at ease. "*
- *"We had a problem with our kitchen floor dipping five inches. We called several floor companies and all said they could fix it but Reinhard found the root of the problem which was basically beam support and fixed it."*

✍ _____

_____

_____

Joseph Ross Building Contractors, (908)668-1285, SC, 20 years in business

Joseph Ross has a compelling portfolio of achievement. He uses an impressive roster of highly-educated professionals with finely honed skills in project management and client communications. The firm specializes in building and remodeling quality homes.

- *"Excellent custom-home builder. Very nice way about him."*
- *"Flexible working with the homeowner."*

✍ _____

_____

_____

J. Rupp Construction, (908)613-8478, SC MIC, 15 years in business

As a general contractor, John Rupp not only does additions and remodeling but can also do custom homes.

- *"He's very creative. Solid construction."*
- *"His work is often complimented on by other construction workers."*
- *"Excellent carpentry and reasonable pricing."*

✍ _____

_____

_____

R. Sagar & R. Tuder Contractors, (732)382-0558, A, 25 years in business

Smaller jobs are preferable to these contractors although they will tackle the big ones. Specialities include roof, gutters, windows and doors, kitchen designs and cabinet installations, porch enclosures and renovations.

- *"They were able to fix a leak from one kitchen window which had us totally baffled."*

- *"They came within a reasonable amount of time and did a great job."*

Jack Taylor Builders, (908)892-8687, A, 25 years in business
This building and development firm specializes in new construction. They concentrate on high quality single-family homes.
- *"He has built two homes for me personally and has built homes for three of my customers (I'm a realtor). All the homes are beautiful."*
- *"He's an honest man that does a quality job. One contract was only a handshake."*

Toddco Construction, (973)376-5889, A, 10 years in business
This is a small contracting company. They do everything from small home repair to larger renovations. The owner is alway on the job with his team to insure that the job is completed to the customer's satisfaction.
- *"An eager beaver, he is very eager to please the customer. He's very personable and all his workmen were absolutely great. We had a water problem in our basement that we could not solve and we replaced the carpet several times. He found the problem and put in new drains. It's perfect now."*
- *"He redid our entire basement and was very reliable. He did every single thing we asked him to do."*

V & J Construction Co. Inc., (908)931-1771, A, 27 years in business
V & J is family-owned. They specialize in plaster restoration and will work on lath and plaster, exterior stucco and decorative moldings. All the staff specialists have beeen together for 13 years and pride themselves on being professional, courteous and clean.
- *"This company does excellent work. They redid plaster in our dining room and reception room. They are very creative—were able to add on missing molding and it was done to perfection. You would never know it was not the original."*
- *"They are nice and considerate of the homeowner. Great when cleaning up. I would have to say overall that they were one of the best contractors we have had work for us ever."*

GILDING

The Gilt Complex, (609)465-4547, A, 18 years in business

Peter Crafts offers a door-to-door gilding service. He will come to a client's home to consult on a piece, take it back to his shop and then return it to the client. He also offers an art conservation and frame restoration service.

- *"I had a mirror that I wanted the frame redone and gilded. He was very honest and said that there was hardly any value to the piece and it was not worth spending my money. I really appreciated this comment."*
- *"He's a real master of his trade. He gilded an antique picture frame for me and it is now the centerpiece of my living room. The frame is more spectacular than the ancestor portrait it holds."*

Restoration of Gilded Antiques, (908)968-5661, A, 10 years in business

Joe Collins, a trained gilder, has a background in art from the Graduate School of Art & Design in Manhattan. All gold-leaf gilding work is meticulously handcrafted. In addition, he will do casting, moldings, and rebuild virtually destroyed antique pieces.

- *"His work is exquisite—as good as the masters of yesteryear."*
- *"I have used him frequently and have never been disappointed."*

Swain Galleries, (908)756-1707, A, 129 years in business

Swain has a reputation for being expert in gold-leaf gilding, gilding repair, and restoration of antique frames. They will make molds and cast or recarve areas wherever parts are missing. Gilding is done in 22-Karat gold leaf, water gilding and burnishing as well as oil gilding and gilding with gold metal leaf.

- *"I recently had an antique mirror frame regilded by Swain. The mirror was quite large and they came to my house to pick it up return it and they rehung it for me. It was a mess but they convinced me it was worth doing. When they delivered it, I could not get over how beautiful it was. It made all the difference in the world. It now occupies a place of honor in my house."*

Allenhurst Stained Glass & Restoration, (732)531-8520, A, 20 years in business

Complete design and restoration of eclesiastical, residential and commercial stained-glass windows is done by this firm.

- *"We had eight leaded-glass windows in our old home that needed much repair. He redid all these windows with old glass. They are done really, really well and there are no drafts."*
- *"He does quality work. He picked all the windows up and took them back to his shop to work on."*

Bissey Glass Works, (732)892-6207, A, 20 years in business

Bissey Glass is a small family-run glass studio that specializes in one-of-a kind stained glass and sandblasted art pieces. These run from front doors to windows to glass tables or sandblasted embellished tabletops. They work for a small number of clients with the goal of producing the finest quality pieces that imagination can dream up.

- *"They installed stained glass in my front door. I adore my door. My friends have given me many compliments. I told him the design I wanted and he laid it out. I chose the colors. Every time I look at his work I love it more."*

Colonial Glass & Mirror Corp., (908)494-2690, A, 10 years in business

This company provides custom mirrors and tabletops for residential and commercial customers.

- *"Our home is almost 100 years old with a lot of things that have to be constantly taken care of. In a hall bathroom is an original beautiful, stained-glass window that was broken in several areas—and it was also weakening. They were able to very artfully repair this window and to brace it."*
- *"He is a really nice guy to deal with and very careful taking care of woodwork around the windows when he installs glass."*

Gorkin Glass Company Inc., (908)756-0544, A, 79 years in business

Gorkin Glass is a family-owned-and-operated business with four generations of design and mechanical knowledge. They install shower doors (⅜"to ½" thick) and framed shower enclosures. In addition they will provide tabletops, all types of mirror work, sandblasting, leaded and etched, carved and decorative glass.

- *"They're great! They do all our glasswork in our home. They installed Plexiglas after our dog broke through our screen door."*
- *"They have made several beveled-glass tabletops for me. They were done to perfection and I have nothing but kudos for this company."*

Livingston Glass Inc., (973)992-2281, UC MC, 19 years in business

Livingston Glass has installed thousands of mirrors in their 19 years of business. They handcraft most of their items including: mirrors, tabletops, shower doors, storms and screens, and sliding bifold mirror doors. Custom-fitting mirror work is an area of their expertise.

- *"He has done small assignments in our home. He repaired glass on large picture frames. He also replaced the mirror that was broken. He has also repaired broken windowpanes."*
- *"He repaired several panes of glass for us and did a beautiful job."*

Metuchen Glass, (908)494-5010, MIC, 22 years in business

Anything done with glass can be done by Metuchen Glass. They provide mirrors and tabletops, but also do Lexan, sliding doors, enclosed patios, Plexiglas, thermopane, plate glass, nonglare and safety glass and storm windows.

- *"They repaired and replaced panes of glass after a very bad storm caused a branch of a tree to go through a window. They did a very nice job . . . were responsive and very reliable."*

Premium Glass, (732)988-1852, A, 46 years in business

Premium Glass specializes in stained glass. They do one-of-a kind glass windows and will also repair and restore existing stained glass. They work with customers to create future heirlooms.

- *"I have a wonderful stained-glass window in my kitchen. Over the years several panes of glass were broken. They repaired and restored my window and it adds so much to the charm of my room. I love it."*

Weather Shield, (908)233-7049, UC, 31 years in business

Friendly, reliable and detail-conscious is the way Weather Shield would like to be known. Their fabrication sizes are extremely accurate and thus render an anxiety-free atmosphere from beginning to end.

- *"Whenever we break glass in a window or storm door, and believe me it happens, they repair it or replace it 1-2-3. They are timely and know what they are doing. They always want to please you."*
- *"Really nice people. I find them so responsive. No one wants to live for very long with a broken window."*

GUTTER INSTALLATION & REPAIR

Komar Roofing, Inc., (908)232-6383, UC, 22 years in business

As part of their comprehensive roofing service, Komar provides gutter cleaning.

- *"They are very good. We have used them many times and they always cleaned up after themselves. If they see any problems they would always let me know so that it could be repaired.*

Landmark Management, (908)654-5803, UC SC, 12 years in business

Landmark is a home-maintenance firm specializing in gutters, deck restoration and house washing. Gutters are installed, cleaned and repaired by a friendly, courteous staff.

- *". . . cleaned our gutters. The best thing about them is that they cleaned up after themselves. Actually, when I called them they came the same day for they were working at my neighbor's house."*
- *"They have cleaned our gutters for four years. They are neat and very good workers. What is nice about them is that they clean up all the garbage and leave no trace of ever having been there."*

Panestakingly Clean, (908)362-6092, A, 22 years in business

How clean do you want your gutters? If you answered Panestakingly Clean you've come to the right company. They pride themselves on prompt service to residential properties, apartment buildings and co-ops.

- *". . . prompt in response to my calls. They are thorough and very polite and reliable."*

Precision Aluminum Inc., (908)499-0814, UC, 18 years in business

This is a siding- and seamless-gutter company that guarantees home owners that they will never clean gutters again. "Gutter Helmet" is guaranteed to keep gutters clean and free-flowing. When a customer calls Precision Aluminum they deal directly with the owner, Bob, who will personally design a solution for all gutter problems.

- *"He installed one gutter helmet for us. He was on schedule, on time and we've had no problems since."*
- *"We love it! Our gutters never have to be cleaned, especially now that my husband is too old to get on a ladder."*

Professional Services MTH, (908)241-4737, UC, 10 years in business

Michael Hoffman, the owner of this company, does preventative maintenance on gutters and roofs. He specializes in storm-damage repairs and leak prevention.

- *"I am very particular of how my gutters are cleaned and he satisfies my needs."*

- *"We use him twice a year and are very pleased with his service."*

Skydell Contracting Inc., (908)271-2938, SC, 9 years in business

Skydell obtained exclusive rights to sell and install Gutter Helmet in Somerset County in 1991. Gutter Helmet is a solid aluminum cover that goes over existing gutters to prevent the buildup of leaves and debris. It is guaranteed to keep gutters and down spouts free-flowing. This company pays individual attention to each project. In addition they are the N.J. distributor for Beaver Basement Water Control Systems.

- *"We chose this company because of the installation of gutter helmet. Now we don't have to have our gutters cleaned. My neighbor used them first and was very pleased so we decided to use them."*
- *". . . very personable."*
- *"These things are great! You never have to clean gutters. They match my roof perfectly and the installers were neat and very nice."*

Ned Stevens Gutter Cleaning, (800)542-0267, A, 32 years in business

This gutter-cleaning and general-contracting firm not only cleans and flushes existing gutters, but will install new gutters, leaders, and gutter screening. They also provide an underground drain service.

- *". . . have used them for six years. They are good because they are very reliable. They come when they say they are."*
- *"You don't have to chase this company. They do good work."*

Watertite Gutters, (732)469-7292, SC, 25 years in business

Watertite is a family business that has been handed down from father to son. They use only the finest quality heavy-gauge aluminum. All installed gutters are seamless and made at the job site. They are installed with a concealed hanging system.

- *"When we first moved to our new home it had aluminum siding. We tore it all off including all the gutters. Watertite replaced every one on the entire house. It was quite a large job. They do excellent work."*
- *"We had damage to two gutters fom one of our sons playing basketball along the side of the house. This was a small job to repair and they came out. I guess what I'm saying is that no job is too small for them."*

HANDYPEOPLE

Benninger & Sons Odd Jobs Co., (908)232-8084, UC, 15 years in business

If a contractor considers a job too small Benninger & Sons is the business to call. They provide personalized service to their customers and go that extra step to assure they are satisfied. Every job is important to them.

- *"It's very difficult to find people to do odd jobs, but they do them in a reliable way."*
- *"They come when they say they are, do a professional job and clean up beautifully."*

Jobs by Patrick, (732)381-9743, UC SC MIC, 30 years in business

This is a small, family-owned "Jack-of-all-trades" business. They will among other things paint, install ceramic tile, do light construction, roofing, build custom decks and do landscaping.

- *". . . just wonderful! They always come whenever I call. They have done a load of different things in my house such as put in molding and fix chairs to name a few."*
- *"I used to call my Dad whenever I needed things done around the house for he was very handy. Now he's not around so I call Patrick. Everyone should have a Patrick."*

Risen Son Home Repair Service, (732)752-6553, MIC, 1 year in business

Paul Fariello is a homeowner's dream—he willingly does all those jobs the average person does not have time to do. These run the gamut from painting and light carpentry to electrical and plumbing-lite. He also has skills in computer repair.

- *"A true Jack-of-all-trades. The nicest guy."*
- *"He recently rag painted a small bathroom for me. We had a terrible mildew problem and he solved it. A pleasure to have in the house."*

John R. Sweeney Painting & Decorating, (973)676-5176, A, 30 years in business

Sweeney is one-stop shopping! In addition to doing minor carpentry and odd jobs he specializes in installing fabric wall coverings. Restoration of older homes is also an area of interest.

- *"Mr. Sweeney is wonderful. He can do anything around the house. We have used him so frequently—he's like family."*

Tru-Handyman, (908)537-9202, UC MC SC, 9 years in business

Jay Trubin has a noble business philosophy: "Do the small job well to get the big jobs; do both size jobs well to keep the customer!" This is a two-man operation concentrating on small carpentry jobs that large companies don't want to do.

- *"He installed a basketball hoop in cement on the driveway. I backed into it twice with the van and he returned each time to fix it—no problem!"*
- *"He has redone all those small jobs that my husband botched!"*

Willy N Renovations, (908)298-8137, A, 15 years in business

Will Moya is a true Mr. Fixit. He repairs and installs locks, Sheetrock, electrical plumbing, roofing, siding, painting and tilework. He prides himself on being organized—even calls before he is coming and if he's going to be late.

- *"He's very nice and so neat he takes his shoes off before coming into my house."*
- *"He's methodical and helps with anything. When he was measuring with my measuring tape, it didn't work so he took it apart and fixed it!"*

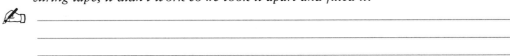

Matt Costello, (908)789-0956, UC, 8 years in business

No job is too small and no job is too large for Matt Costello. With a variety of sized trucks available, Matt says he will come at the "drop of a hat" for last-minute callers.

- *"Nothing is a problem. He will haul away anything."*
- *"He gets rid of all junk. A really nice guy—great personality."*

Gary Flannery Construction Inc., (732)752-2514, A, 22 years in business

Flannery Construction closely customizes their service to each customer. They do demolition, cleanup and haul construction debris.

- *"He did a good job. Was very dependable and I would use him again."*

J & R Services Inc., (908)686-5229, UC, 5 years in business

J & R is a rubbish-removal company specializing in residential- and commercial-debris removal. They also provide a dumpster service as well as interior and exterior demolition for homeowners.

- *"They were neat and efficient—very thorough."*
- *"They did all the hauling for our addition. A very nice person."*

Phil's General Hauling, (908)757-0288, UC SC MIC, 21 years in business

Phil Beverly calls himself a "cartman." He will personally cart away whatever castoffs or objects the customer no longer wants.

- *"He's very efficient and can take just about anything and toss it out."*
- *"He has big, strong workmen, so it is not a problem getting rid of construction debris or emptying out your basement or attic."*

Pinto Brothers Disposal, (908)561-8231, UC SC MIC, 16 years in business

For 16 years Pinto has been hauling, disposing and recycling for industrial, residential and commercial properties. They have a container service for 1 to 50 yards.

- *"They have hauled trash for us. They're very efficient and cooperative. I would definitely use them again whenever needed."*

Preferred Maintenance & Carting Inc., (908)232-4094, UC SC MIC, 13 years in business

Service is a priority to this company. They haul containers (1 to 40 yards) and do cleanups.

HAULERS

- *"We have used him for both commercial and residential. He's nice . . . very personable and willing to please. He's dependable. All I have to do is ask and he just does."*
- *"We frequently have large parties in our home and we use him to take away many items to be discarded."*

Prendeville Industries Inc., (800)635-8816, UC MC SC, 22 years in business

They do the work that others will not or do not want to do. This includes: cleaning out attics, basements, garage, yards; cleanup and rubbish removal; waste removal; unwanted items and bulky items. Dumpsters are available.

- *"A very nice man. I felt comfortable working with him. He came when he said he would. He hauled away rock-debris, very heavy stuff that we were unable to do ourselves."*
- *"He cleaned up our driveway of leftover debris before he left the job."*
- *"We used him twice and would definitely use him again. I would recommend him to anyone especially if they need heavy things hauled away."*

Reliant Waste & Recycling Services, (888)7RELIANT, A, 2 years in business

Reliant is a full-service waste management company, catering to homeowners and small businesses. Their efforts are concentrated on recycling as opposed to landfilling. Container sizes are available from 2 to 40 yards.

- *"This is a fairly new company that is willing to help you in any way. They have big trucks, dump trucks, dumpsters and just about anything for commercial or residential. A really nice guy."*

INTERIOR DECORATORS

Benjamin Interiors, (973)379-4894, UC MC, 3 years in business

Sharon Klesse has been involved in the fine arts as a teacher and designer for many years. She actively assists her clients in space planning which ultimately involve floor plans. She is also involved with furniture selection, window-treatment design and fabrication, choosing fabrics and wallcoverings and arranging decorative lighting. Advice is also available on flooring and fixtures.

- *"Sharon has the talent to make a room a liveable and functional space. She has the ability to take the conceptual stage of design and drawing to the detailed finished product. She's very good!"*

Carriage House Interiors, (908)781-5740, MC SC, 4 years in business

This decorator works closely with her clients by guiding them but not overwhelming them. She loves to use their furniture to create a "true" home for her clients.

- *"Her own home speaks for what a great decorator she is. It's traditional and classic with lots of pizazz added. She has done work for several friends of mine and everything is just beautiful."*

Susan Cleary Interiors, (908)232-4644, A, 12 years in business

Creating comfortable and unique spaces to fit the customer's lifestyle is what Susan Cleary wants to accomplish. A customer can use her interior-design expertise in window treatments, custom-reupholstery and space planning.

- *"We used Susan several years ago for upholstery of antique furniture. She is extremely conscientious and very willing to please. She is very responsive to phone calls."*
- *"We were redoing our family room and needed new window treatments. Plus our furniture needed reupholstering. Susan was able to get it done in a reasonable amount of time. It looks lovely and her selection of fabrics was quite good."*

Sandra D'Amata Inc., (973)763-1070, A, 25 years in business

This interior designer's expertise is very broad and varied. After having worked at Bloomingdale's and Sloane's in Beverly Hills, she established her own business. Her staff, which has been with her for many years is well-skilled and qualified in all areas of design. They will work with the present rooms in a client's home and create color schemes, select and purchase furnishings, draw detailed floor plans and arrange New York shopping trips. They also will assist the customer during renovation or new construction. Accessory consulting is also available.

INTERIOR DECORATORS

99

• *"She does 'drop dead' gorgeous work. The highest of high-end decorators that I am aware of. She is creative with putting together carpet, fabrics and color."*

Maureen Foley Interiors, (908)889-7600, UC SC WC, 6 years in business

Maureen brings a level of financial expertise to her business which is always comforting to clients. She views the project in its entirety, thereby assuring that resources are available to complete the picture, such as accessories. Existing furniture, rugs, and art work are incorporated because these are frequently important to the client. Various scenarios are offered for each project. That way a client knows what is "in" or "trendy" and what has timeless appeal.

• *"She spent one-and-one-half years helping me decorate my home. She is delightful to work with, not at all pushy, and she spends as much time as is needed."*
• *"... helped me choose my carpeting, upholstery and window treatments. She did a great job and I would recommend her to anyone."*

Elizabeth B. Gillin Interiors, (908)654-9376, A, 23 years in business

This award-winning interior designer has a full-service firm. A good portion of her work experience has come from working at Bloomingdale's in New York City for 10 years as a store designer. Presently she will do renovations, kitchens, architectural detailing, total room or home design and installations. Commercial interior design is also available.

• *"I was in charge of a showcase home and Beth decorated a room just for children. It was the kind of room that once you saw it you would always remember how special it was. The fabrics she used were fabulous and she mixed antiques with the new. This room was loved and 'oohed and aahed' by everyone. She really is a talent!"*

Greenbaum Interiors, (973)279-3000, A, 45 years in business

Greenbaum has a staff of experienced interior designers who are trained to guide the customer in space planning, coordinating color, fabric and floor covering schemes, designing wall and window treatments and adding final decorative touches to help make the home gracious, comfortable and refined.

• *"I think they are just fabulous! They do everything (absolutely everything). They did my entire living room and some other things in adjacent rooms to maintain the flow. This is what I mean about offering a complete service."*
• *"They are very accommodating and will do anything in terms of design. They will*

loan you things and you can live with them for a while after which you can buy or return them. They have the most interesting pieces in their store—very upscale. They are great!"

✍ _____

_____

_____

L'Egid Limited Interior Design, (212)737-0011, A, 30 years in business

The first visit to any customer from L'Egid will usually last at least two hours and will be free of charge. It is a time to learn about the customer's needs, lifestyle and taste. A great effort is made to provide a stress-free environment for the customer and make the whole experience pleasant, easy and a wonderful learning experience.

- *"I have been working with L'Egid for about two years. They have done everything in my home from window treatments to furniture and we love everything. They are pleasant and dependable and most of all they stand behind their subcontractors."*

✍ _____

_____

_____

La Jolie Maison, (908)598-7170, UC MC SC WC, 20 years in business

This is a full interior-design firm that will work with their clients from preconstruction to the final details. They have seven interior designers on staff and all are very experienced. From contemporary to classic traditional, they can help the customer with all needs. When you call, ask about visiting their showroom which is truly a showcase of their work.

- *"I chose them for they are very experienced. They can handle any design. They are very nice to work with."*
- *"They decorated my daughter's bedroom with wonderful fabrics, a tent ceiling and carpeting. My daughter was thrilled with her new room."*
- *"They redid our den from furniture to fabric on the walls and carpeting. My husband and I so enjoy this room now."*

✍ _____

_____

_____

Lang, Winslow & Smith Co., (973)635-2719, A, 30 years in business

After many years of creating exciting interiors for clients across the country, this firm has enhanced their design practice by incorporating the added dimension of feng shui. Feng shui is the study of the way in which environment affects our health, wealth, and personal happiness. This ancient Chinese art of placement and design has become increasingly popular in the U.S. Donna Lang and Vincent Smith will analyze the flow of energy in your home or office and design an interior to suit the client.

- *". . . very gifted and creative. Donna is a neat person. She had just published several books on decorating. I have worked with her on several projects and there were times that these projects were driving me crazy. Donna was great—she never loses her cool."*

- *"They know how to plan a room just perfectly. Anyone who uses them should be very pleased."*

Lexis Associates Inc., (732)563-4111, MC SC, 20 years in business

Lexis Associates is a professional design firm with a staff of six persons. They specialize in working with clients and specific budgets to create a wonderful interior. Their staff is all schooled professionals with degrees in design and have the expertise to carry out a project in a timely fashion.

- *"They are a creative and diverse design firm. They designed several model homes for us and their interiors attracted attention and interest among all the prospective home buyers."*

Jean M. Mountford Interior Design, (973)377-9309, A, 11 years in business

Jean Mountford is a rarity. She designs, sews and installs window treatments, table covers, pillows, cushions and dust ruffles. She also deals in art, antiques and Oriental carpets. In addition, she will advise on furniture, carpets, wallpaper, paint color and accessories.

- *"She has been my decorator for three years. She's done almost every room in my home. I love the reaction I get from people when they come to my home. They all ask who has done the decorating for it's so beautiful."*
- *"She did my husband's office. I find her to be creative, quick and efficient."*

Marilyn Norton Interiors, (908)233-2520, A, 8 years in business

Reflecting the client's taste and lifestyle in interior decorating is of primary importance to Marilyn Norton. She will skillfully guide her customers in the selection of furniture, accessories, window treatments, wallpaper and fabric selection. Her guidance is important but she emphasizes that the final approval and decision rests with the client.

- *"She is cheerful and easy to work with."*
- *"She's an outstanding talent with creative ideas."*

Patterson Interiors, (908)518-0102, A, 7 years in business

A degree in textile and interior design makes this decorator well-qualified to satisfy customer needs. She will come to your home by appointment and give you ideas for windows, upholstering, fabrics, wallcoverings and accessories.

- *"Jan has a wonderful eye for color and accessorizing. A real plus is to go into her store which is in a lovely older home. All the rooms are set up beautifully to give an idea of how she decorates. We like her very much."*

- *"Jan is the sweetest, nicest person. She has been extremely helpful to me in choosing fabrics for my dining room and window treatments. Her store is lovely and the people that work for her are just delightful."*

 _____

_____

Pereaux Interior Design, (973)993-8255, A, 20 years in business

Pereaux occupies two traditional furniture design studios. A customer is provided a full service of design needs from traditional to transitional.

- *"They are wonderful! Their storefronts are fabulous. I worked with Dennis Fischbach and he is really outstanding, nice, and a fabulous decorator. He's highly intuitive."*
- *"Dennis is the kind of person that you can give ideas or pictures to and he will come up with many different alternatives. Every detail is taken care of; nothing is left to surprise. Everything is perfect! Our money was well-spent."*

 _____

_____

Mary Fitzpatrick Richardson Interiors, (732)295-8582, A, 25 years in business

Mary Richardson's main objective is to maintain the character of her clients in all design work. Her experience as an artist has enabled her to be especially expert with color. Mixing old with the new effectively is a true love of hers.

- *"She is exceptionally creative and a wonderful decorator. In addition she is an absolutely lovely person."*
- *"Her own home is a true showcase of the fabulous work she does. She is also quite an artist, so she has an eye for color."*

 _____

_____

Theresa Ann Scelfo, (973)379-8945, A, 10 years in business

With over 10 years of experience in both residential and commercial design, Terri combines the experience with the ability to listen, develop and design for the client's individual needs.

- *"We just love Terri! She is patient and accommodating. She's easy to work with and will not give you a lot of pressure. She did my husband's office which was a huge job and it looks great."*
- *"She chose fabrics for my living room and helped me to choose an Oriental rug. I like her for she is very diversified in her style—contemporary to traditional."*

_____

_____

Sleepy Hollow Interiors, (908)753-4089, A, 6 years in business

Sleepy Hollow Interiors strives to create a beautiful finished product that is comfortable, long-lasting and reflective of individual taste. All pressure is taken off the customer when employing this firm for they do everything from designing to installing and providing expert coordination for the entire project.

- *"I came to know Darlene (owner of Sleepy Hollow) in a funny way. I won her*

INTERIOR DECORATORS

services in a silent auction. It was the best thing I have ever won! She came to my house and advised us on what we should do overall. She had absolutely fabulous ideas. I have subsequently seen her work and I can truly say she is very good."

- *"She is one of the loveliest people you'd ever want to meet. A very creative decorator."*

Gail Taenzler Inc., (973)762-2131, A, 28 years in business

This design firm specializes in extensive interior architectural renovations. They handle all aspects of design projects from conception, production of drawings, through construction supervision. Design style ranges from traditional to ultracontemporary with emphasis on creating unique environments tailored to the client. Custom cabinetry, furniture and upholstery can also be designed for each project.

- *"Gail helped me when we moved into our new house. She designed our living room, dining room and library. I found that the best thing about her was that she listened and adapted her designs to fit our lifestyle. We are so pleased with these rooms."*

The Taylors, (908)654-6018, A, 18 years in business

Maggie Taylor specializes in traditional interior design. She believes a home should be warm, comfortable and inviting. The personalities, lifestyle and taste of those who live there should be reflected in every room. She also believes that creating a special environment comes from establishing a personal, relaxed relationship with each client.

- *"I have worked with Maggie on two occasions, which were showhouses. One room was a man's study done in paisleys—really sensational! The second room was an extremely large living room—again stunning."*
- *"She is traditional in her feel and loves the old-fashioned look of rugs as well. She has a knack for doing intimate rooms."*
- *"We used Maggie for a very pretty window area in my second-floor hallway. We knew the look we wanted but had been struggling with ideas for a few years. Maggie pulled the whole hallway together and it looks fabulous. She's a real genius and a lovely person combined."*

KITCHEN & BATH

Albecker's Kitchens & Baths, (732)251-2745, A, 41 years in business
John Albecker puts the customer's remodeling ideas and dreams into reality. With 40-plus years in the business, they have a division to handle kitchen and bathroom designing, planning and installation. Their professional staff can help save time and aggravation by controlling the job from conception to completion. This prevents costly mistakes that occur when several contractors are involved.
- *"Albecker's did our kitchen. They did a very nice job of listening to our needs and following through exactly. They do all the work themselves and do not subcontract. The job was completed in the time they had said. I spend a lot of time in the kitchen and now the surroundings are very pleasant."*

Arrow Crafts, (973)887-6917, MC SC, 35 years in business
Arrow Crafts has been a full-service kitchen and bath dealer for over 30 years. They offer the most complete design, planning, installation and service available. Their association with Rutt Custom Cabinetry has enabled Arrow Crafts to porduce designs that truly reflect the lifestyles of their clients.
- *"They do great design work in the kitchen. They worked well with the subcontractors and they are excellent craftsmen."*
- *"They were very fussy when installing my kitchen countertops to make sure the lines and spaces were perfect."*

The Bath Connection, (973)467-7888, A, 11 years in business
Planning the perfect, functional bathroom or kitchen for any budget is the goal of The Bath Connection. Their primary specialty is the sale of plumbing products, but they also provide a personalized design service.
- *"Their sales help is fabulous. We did major renovations on our home and purchased all our bath accessories from them. They coordinated all our colors and gave us very good advice."*

BBJ Inc., (908)356-7441, A, 15 years in business
BBJ is a full-service remodeling firm with considerable experience in all phases of construction including kitchen and bath. Design guidance and product selection expertise assures the homeowner that the project will be within budget.
- *"BBJ completely redid our guest bathroom. They did a superb job, a phenomenal job. They came on schedule and stayed until the work was done."*
- *"They just completed work on remodeling my kitchen. They worked closely with us to design the perfect kitchen for our needs. My husband is an amateur gourmet cook and had many specific requirements he wanted satisfied. No matter how*

odd they thought his needs were, they worked very hard to design a kitchen that he could use and be proud of. They were successful, we love it."

Beautiful Kitchens & Cabinetry, (732)388-2552, A, 34 years in business

The owner of this company is an award-winning designer of the American Institute of Kitchen Dealers' Kitchen Design Award. He will design, remodel and install cabinetry and whole kitchens.

- *"We lived for many years complaining about our tired, old kitchen. We began to look around for someone to gut and reconstruct and we decided that Beautiful Kitchens would be best for us. They built a 'beautiful kitchen' that we love and is totally serviceable and most of all—totally us."*

Beautiful Kitchens & Cabinetry at Romance Interiors, (908)789-1828, UC MC WC, 11 years in business

Eight years of hotel kitchen design have prepared Mila Dietze in her business. She designs and sells custom wood cabinetry.

- *"Mila is extremely creative. She is designing cabinets for us and I am amazed at her level of expertise and attention to detail. She is a perfectionist but not a driven 'A' personality type. Very easy to work with."*

Beauty Craft Kitchens & Baths Inc., (732)968-6757, UC SC, 40 years in business

Designing and installing the complete kitchen and bath and insuring that the customer's needs are taken into consideration are the project goals of this business. Experienced professionals treat everyone with respect and no wish is beyond considering. They present many planned options so that the customer feels absolutely comfortable with the final best choice.

- *"A very personable, friendly family business. They work closely with you and keep good 'tabs' on the job. They met our deadlines. Quality craftsmen."*
- *"They did our entire kitchen and powder room. They also spruced up three upstairs bathrooms. They gutted our kitchen—did all the plumbing, electrical, carpentry in a very timely fashion. They have good design ideas and beautiful workmanship. They have excellent taste and I would recommend them highly."*

Distinctive Renovations, Inc., (732)280-2288, A, 15 years in business

Distinctive Renovations provides "one-stop shopping" for kitchen and bath remodeling. They are a general contractor for all design services, custom and semicustom cabinetry, countertops, custom tile, electrical requirements, plumbing changes and carpentry.

- *"They completely renovated a very large bathroom. We were very happy with the end result. They are methodical and did the actual designing with us."*

- *"They are very pleasant and nice . . . trustworthy. Great helpful ideas and wonderful to work with."*

✎ _____

_____

Dudick & Son, (908)789-1790, UC MC SC MIC, 50 years in business

Dudick specializes in complete kitchen and bathroom remodeling. Design and product selection is done in their showroom. They do the complete job—no subcontractors.

- *"Dudick has put in two kitchens in two different homes for me. In my third home he redid the front of the kitchen cabinet doors. He resurfaced vanities in our bathrooms. They have good solid products and good quality craftsmanship."*
- *"They will come back—even a year or two later—if you should experience a problem. They are a reliable business that has been around for a long time."*

✎ _____

_____

I Q Construction, (973)467-4473, MC SC, 15 years in business

David Johnson combines his skills as an artist with his skills as a craftsman to create appropriately detailed spaces. His efforts go into designing a room that ultimately looks and is completely compatible and comfortable with the customer's lifestyle.

- *"He is so creative. He did ceramic tile in our bathroom that is beautiful. He is significantly sensitive to older homes. He also put in a new kitchen for our neighbor and it is just magnificent."*

✎ _____

_____

JoAnne's Kitchens, (908)561-5045, A, 50+ years in business

Working in their own shop, JoAnne's provides the customer with expert craftsmanship in the building of custom cabinets. Their designs are drawn by hand so they suit the customer's needs.

- *"Very fine quality and high-grade work. They are service-oriented and deliver when they say they will."*

✎ _____

_____

Lindex Construction Co., (908)756-1455, A, 16 years in business

Lindex takes pride in treating your home as if it were their own. Under no circumstances are any corners cut and the customer's satisfaction is their ultimate goal.

- *"My husband's bathroom was a total disaster. He was happy with it for it reminded him of his bathroom in his dorm in college (you get the picture). I finally convinced him it had to be redone. They installed a bathroom for him which is functional and he is thrilled with it. Very, very good job."*

✎ _____

_____

Pastiche, Inc., (732)447-3322, MC SC, 2 years in business

Even though this firm has only been in business for two years they have 45 years of experience in the field of kitchen design. They will design new and redesign old kitchens and also do remodeling including additions and alterations.

- *"They are truly nice to deal with. They redid a kitchen cabinet that had been broken in shipping. They did specialty custom cabinets for our kitchen and installed an architectural ceiling. A truly beautiful job."*
- *"The doorways going into our kitchen were quite plain and he changed them to arched doorways with columns. He helped make a new home have an old-fashioned look. We would use him over and over again because he does pure quality work."*

Proven Design, Inc., (908)245-1090, A, 38 years in business

Custom cabinets from Proven Design are solidly constructed using only the finest materials and latest machinery and tools. Their highly skilled cabinetmakers take great pride in their work crafting each kitchen to the customer's design specifications and taste. They have their own cabinet shop which lets the customer personalize every room in the house. Stylish, innovative storage solutions that are functional and durable are also offered.

- *"Our kitchen was designed 18 years ago and is still as lovely and functional as day one. Proven Design obviously takes pride in fine craftsmanship and detail. They maintain their reputation with satisfied customers like me."*

Royal Cabinet Company Inc., (800)834-8920, A, 35 years in business

This custom cabinet manufacturer does kitchens, home offices, libraries and vanities. An engineering department helps make even the most complicated projects manageable.

- *"We have a new home which was custom-built. Royal installed the kitchen, bathroom and library cabinets. They did good work and use quality material. They provide an excellent service."*
- *"They build beautiful cabinets. A vanity was constructed by them in my sister-in-law's house and they did a beautiful job. Easy to work with."*

Stonehouse Designs, (908)781-8384, A, 2 years in business

Stonehouse Design will guide the client to help them realize their home's potential. From powder room to kitchen they create designs that are both functional, warm and welcoming. Every style from contemporary to traditional is offered and Claudia Harvey has an extensive knowledge of carpentry, tile and stone which will help to make the client's decisions benefit the existing space.

- *"Claudia helped me enormously when we redid our kitchen two years ago. She helped select the tiles and the design, the brass knobs for the cabinet doors and the granite countertops. She's very knowledgeable and a lovely person—extremely* easy to work with. She always returned my phone calls and I would highly recommend her!"

_____
_____
_____

Superior Custom Kitchens, (908)753-6005, A, 30 years in business

As one of New Jersey's oldest kitchen dealers, Superior will design and manufacture to the customer's requirements. They pride themselves on providing even the most unusual and hard-to-fit cabinets.

- *"Very good and dependable. You can tell he has been doing this for years for it shows in our kitchen. Every crew that was in (demolition, tile and cabinets) were all well-coordinated so that the end result was beautiful and done in six weeks. I have heard so many horror stories about redoing kitchens but with Jack this was not so. I have nothing but praise and if we were to do another kitchen it would be with Superior."*

_____
_____
_____

Toddco Construction, (973)376-5889, A, 10 years in business

The owner of this small contracting company is on-the-job of every kitchen and bath renovation. He will answer any questions that any of his clients may have regarding the job.

- *"This guy is such a go-getter and a really nice guy. He does really high-quality work and can build anything. Great eye for details."*

_____
_____
_____

Walls & Door, Inc., (908)968-8988, UC SC MIC, 16 years in business

With an inventory of approximately 300 units, the consumer should not have a problem picking out shower doors from this company. They install the doors and if the opening is already there, they will build around it.

- *"They are reputable and accommodating. We had two bathrooms renovated and they installed the shower doors and did a wonderful job."*
- *"They are great—truly helpful. They installed our shower doors and a number of years later when we had a problem, they responded quickly and fixed it to our satisfaction."*

_____
_____
_____

LANDSCAPE DESIGN

All American Landscape, (908)276-1891, UC MC SC, 10 years in business

This company feels it is different from others because they provide a package of services which saves the consumer from hiring several firms for landscape management. They are licensed by the NJ DEP for chemical applications for turf and shrubs.

- *"This is a very efficient way of maintaining my property. They not only handle the creative work but do general maintenance work also."*

Bataille Land Design, (908)730-7299, A, 16 years in business

Gergory E. Bataille is a New Jersey Certified Landscape architect who specializes in fine residential and commercial site-design and master planning. His projects range from the intimacy of a small water garden or patio space to the grandness of a public park. Bataille pays particular attention to detail when creating designs. Important aspects of his residential design include creating outdoor living and entertaining spaces incorporating sculptures, patios and decks, rock walls, swimming pools, ponds and waterfalls, pergolas and trellises.

- *"His scope is very broad. He worked with Park Systems of Carolinas. He's good for incorporation of natural topography and geographical elements of the land."*
- *"He's done award-winning gardens."*

Blue Meadow Landscape Architects, (201)891-4386, A, 20 years in business

This award-winning design firm concentrates on developing the surrounding landscape to complement the architectural styles and features of the residence. They are widely known for their professional execution of informal and formal landscape design and garden restoration and for use of water in the garden.

- *". . . very creative, professional, knowledgeable and unique."*
- *"They have a beautiful approach to landscaping by taking into consideration the type of home and custom-designing a garden that optimizes the features of the residence."*

Brandner Nursery, (908)879-6577, UC MC SC WC, 13 years in business

This nursery endeavors to provide unusual varieties and materials of plants and flowers. They specialize in Bonsai trees and have many displays of water gardens and stonework on their property. A Landscape Design division strives to create landscapes unique to the customer which will enhance their property while not breaking the budget.

- *"These people are very creative. They transformed old, tired gardens on my property into a wondrous place that we are proud to show off."*

_____

Bravo Landscape Construction, (908)322-4678, A, 11 years in business

A professional landscape can increase the market value of a home by as much as 23% and Bravo believes that a beautifully landscaped home should reflect the owner's personality. They will provide customized designs and have extensive knowledge of standard plants, annuals and perennials, organic orchards, waterplants and rose gardens.

- *"They can transform anything into a thing of beauty."*
- *"They do beautiful landscaping on small properties . . . and large too."*
- *"He really listens to what I want and suggests the appropriate plantings for each area."*

_____
_____
_____

Cavagnaro Nursery & Landscaping, (908)369-5899, SC, 15 years in business

This landscaping company provides all phases of design and installation. They will do foundation plantings, designer walks and patios, poolscapes, perennial beds and landscape renovations. They have also acquired an expertise in garden and path lighting.

- *"They do quality work . . . excellent. They stand behind their work."*
- *". . . has done specimen plantings at my home and everything is thriving beautifully. I have seen his home which is truly a showcase of his expertise in planting."*

_____
_____
_____

Custom Landscape Systems, Inc., (732)549-1650, A, 20 years in business

This landscape design firm creates original designs to satisfy the requirements of their clients. Special attention is paid to artistically incorporating existing elements of the garden to blend with new plantings.

- *"They are very creative with design. He is a natural artist and has a real feel for the customer's needs."*
- *"They are very observant of the yard and what they want it ultimately to look like."*
- *"He's a fortune-teller. He can see what the garden will look like 20 years down the road."*

_____
_____

T.W. Fish Landscape Nurseryman Inc., (908)464-3807, UC MC, 20 years in business

Tom Fish calls himself a "Landscape-Nurseryman." He emphasizes the proper selection and spacing of plants plus naturalistic hand-pruning/thinning out of small trees, shrubbery and evergreens. As a nurseryman, he can diagnose and treat many pest problems.

111

- *"Plants are his life. He is really, really, really knowledgeable."*
- *"No job is too big or too small."*

_____
_____
_____

Foerster Landscape Inc., (973)584-6674, MC SC, 19 years in business

This is a full-service landscape company that designs, builds and maintains properties. They oversee each job from start to finish.

- *"They are wonderful for property maintenance—do everything from soup to nuts."*
- *"They are professional and knowledgeable. They are good with planting deer-resistant plants."*

_____
_____
_____

From the Ground Up, (908)766-9375, A, 3 years in business

Master planners of the great gardens of the world probably did not have to consider where to place the trash barrels or how to hide a neighbor's unattractive fence. This firm tackles those problems. The owner, Helen Walton, was a curator at the herbarium at the New York Botanical Gardens. Her knowledge of plants and their habitats in concert with her experience in interior design and architecture gives her the ability to create a seamless environment from inside to outdoors.

- *"Helen is a true artist! Her ability to recognize a problem and create a solution that will be long-lasting and unique is astounding. Our garden is now a showplace that we can maintain and be proud of. She is the best!"*

_____
_____
_____

Manheimer/Hertzog Ltd., (609)397-1454, SC WC, 16 years in business

As a landscape design service, they will integrate architectural elements into functional interesting outdoor environments. Their strong use of herbaceous material has always been a trademark of their work.

- *"Absolutely fabulous! They have done all our design work and maintain all our plantings. Every year they plant our pots and do them for change of seasons. They have also done trimming."*
- *"They are very knowledgeable and pleasant to deal with. They're great with giving us helpful tips to maintain everything. We highly recommend them!"*

_____
_____
_____

Miller Landscape Services, Inc., (908)284-0693, A, 7 years in business

Miller Landscape Services owns a 40-acre nursery where they grow ornamental grasses, perennials, trees, shrubs and exotic plantings. Their degreed professionals specialize in ornamental horticulture and environmental design. A special plus is state-of-the-art computer imaging which will transform a 35mm-colored photograph into a realistic image of the future landscape before any work has been started.

- *"They did major landscaping. They were very professional and achieved the look we wanted."*

✍ _____

_____

_____

Murphy Landscaping, (908)769-8277, UC MC SC, 4 years in business

If you are looking for a full-service landscape company perhaps Murphy landscaping could satisfy your needs. Their services include landscape design, installation and maintenance, walkways, tree removal, plantings, stump grinding, mulch, retaining walls and French drains.

- *". . . dependable, creative."*
- *"They re-landscaped the front lawn. Provided excellent follow-up."*
- *"He's a good listener, very knowledgeable and had a wonderful guarantee I was pleased with."*

✍ _____

_____

_____

Osterman Nursery, (908)369-4600, MC SC MIC, 83 years in business

Are you particularly bothered by "out-of-date" landscapes? Ken Osterman is the man to call. He specializes in renovating older properties mostly with larger-size plant material. Ninety percent of material is grown on his 250-acre farm in Somerset County. An additional benefit is his proven expertise in tasteful landscape lighting.

- *"He transformed our old, overgrown property into a Shangri-la."*
- *"He redesigned an old gazebo into something we now use for lovely, summer entertaining."*

✍ _____

_____

_____

Peter Ritchie & Associates, (609)924-4003, A, 16 years in business

This award-winning landscape architecture firm creates environmentally sound and people-friendly designs for residential, corporate or commercial properties. Project scale ranges from very small to large and urban, suburban or rural.

- *". . . does really neat stuff."*
- *"He provides nicely chosen shrubs and works well with problem at hand."*

✍ _____

_____

John Charles Smith & Associates, (908)234-1121, A, 32 years in business

Specializing in landscape architecture for both residential and commercial properties, this

LAWN & TREE MAINTENANCE

- *"I am very particular and they did an extremely professional job removing trees from my property."*

✍ _____

_____

C.H.E.A.P. Tree Experts, (732)548-1653, MIC, 15 years in business

"Try us—you won't be sorry" is the motto of this tree company. As their name implies, they strive to make their service very appealing to customers.

- *"They are quick and efficient. We have used them for seven to eight years and they have done a good job. They clean up well."*

✍ _____

_____

Davey Tree Expert Co., (973)386-1334, UC SC MC, 110 years in business

An employee-owned company, Davey Tree has their own research and development center with arborists on staff.

- *"They are prompt and very thorough."*

✍ _____

_____

Peter Ellis Tree Service, (908)245-1203, UC, 25 years in business

When nature needs a little help, let it be from Pete Ellis Tree Service. As a small business, they take pride in their work which ranges from tree service, removal and trimming to feeding, planting, pruning, snowplowing and stump removal. A 100-foot crane for hire is another service.

- *"They cut down and trimmed trees for us. They also dug out stumps. They're very good to work with."*

✍ _____

_____

_____

Fairway Green, Inc., (908)281-7888, SC, 10 years in business

This locally owned company provides professional lawn, tree/shrub, and insect-control service. Their highly trained staff uses quality products (including organic products) and offers a 100% guarantee on all treatments.

- *". . . really, really dependable."*
- *"They do everything to please the customer and our lawn looks great!"*

✍ _____

_____

_____

Duncan Foster Tree Service, (973)379-3710, UC, 30 years in business

Duncan Foster is a full-service tree and landscaping company. They specialize in fertilization, removals, pruning, stump grinding, cabling and firewood. They will also design landscapes and plant.

- *"Duncan knows everything about trees. Sometimes we think he talks to the trees—*

they do so well after his care. In his own way he is extremely effective with what he does."

_____

_____

Garden Coast Landscaping Inc., (973)377-9370, UC MC SC MIC, 17 years in business
This complete landscaping service does design and maintenance. They will sod, mulch and put down topsoil and decorative stones. Nine- and twelve-month maintenance service contracts are offered.

- *". . . have used him for a number of years. Very dependable. He mows our lawn and does some of the planting. He's just a dependable, reliable guy."*

_____

_____

_____

Joseph's Landscaping, (973)644-3443, A, 6 years in business
This family-owned company provides standard landscaping and maintenance. Weekly programs include: cleanups, thatching, seeding, weeding and insect and disease control.

- *". . . extremely hardworking. Great guy. His sons work with him and they do a terrific job."*
- *"Very experienced."*
- *"He's very good maintaining properties of old homes with mature plantings."*

_____

_____

_____

Kennedy Landscaping Inc., (908)396-9868, UC MIC, 15 years in business
The customer that uses this lawn-care and landscape company is assured that a custom maintenance program will be designed for them. Their emphasis is on healthy soil which results in healthier plants and less use of pesticides.

- *"We have used this company for several years and the results are wonderful. Our lawn has never looked better!"*

_____

_____

_____

Joseph Lefano Landscaping & Maintenance, (908)245-8863, UC, 30 years in business
Starting out with one man and one truck, this business has grown in a few years to a thriving landscape company. They offer numerous services to their customers from landscaping and maintenance to drainage work, driveway curbing, patios and sidewalks, pavers, railroad ties, retaining walls and snowplowing. "One-stop shopping" for all your outdoor needs!

- *". . . very reliable. He is a perfectionist."*
- *"He has been mowing, weeding and doing our fall cleanups for years."*

_____

_____

LAWN & TREE MAINTENANCE

Martoccia Landscaping, (908)755-6585, UC SC, 35 years in business

Tony Martoccia works primarily on residential landscape maintenance. In addition to standard lawn maintenance, he will do thatching, aeration, fertilization, seeding and insect and disease control. His tree service provides removal, pruning, grinding and feeding. Other services are snowplowing and gutter cleaning.

- *"Tony is extremely reliable. He's been known to come in the dead of night or early morning for emergencies."*
- *"He's a real perfectionist. A self-starter, he anticipates my needs before I even know I need it."*

Nelson Tree Service Inc., (908)757-7243, A, 23 years in business

This is a full-service tree company that does trimming, cabling and removals (trees and stumps). Land clearing and emergency storm-damage repair are also provided.

- *"We tried other tree guys , but I think this guy is great. He responds quickly. He has done sidewalk root-pruning of our trees and did some guying of one of our trees."*

Prisco Associates Landscapes, (732)469-8948, MC SC MIC WC, 5 years in business

Prisco is an owner-operated firm providing lawn maintenance and tree work. Services include: pruning, shrub trimming, seeding and sodding, landscape design and installation, mulching and stonework. They also provide a complete snow-removal service.

- *"Reliable, extremely polite and easy to deal with."*

M. Romano & Son Landscaping & Paving, (908)789-2293, UC, 29 years in business

Quality of workmanship and materials are the primary focus of the Romanos. Being in the business for three decades their name is well-known in the areas they service.

- *"They maintain my property beautifully. They do fall and spring cleanups to perfection and are willing to do anything I ask. They are very dependable."*

Schengrund Landscaping & Tree Service, (908)753-2299, A, 13 years in business

If the homeowner is shopping for a "new look" for their landscape, Mike Schengrund is their man. He will provide just the right plants to match soil conditions, seasonal changes and whatever other requirements the customer has. Tree service is also included.

- *". . . very pleasant."*

- *"He's a real perfectionist to the point that the mower lines on the grass are always straight and even."*

✍ _____

John Sellino & Sons, (908)754-5159, UC, 20 years in business

Even though Sellino considers themselves a landscape and maintenance firm, they also do landscape design, dry-stone walls, trimming pruning and should you want a fish pond—they'll do it!
- *"He's fabulous. We have used him for 10 years."*
- *"He has meticulous workers. They maintain our property including our shrubs. They do our fall and spring cleanups. He also installed our flower beds."*

✍ _____

Tamke Tree Experts, Inc., (800)822-3537, A, 30 years in business

This company is "one-stop shopping" for all areas of tree care and maintenance. Arboriculture is a very scientific field and company representatives are routinely encouraged to attend conventions and seminars around the country to keep abreast of the latest treatments. Use of technology includes a new computer system to keep track of clients' valuable trees.
- *"They do all my spraying. They are extremely knowledgeable and very accommodating."*

✍ _____

Tree Tech/Lawn Tech Inc., (800)327-0034, A, 21 years in business

As horticulturists, they specialize in lawn care, disease and insect control, pruning, and tree removal. They pride themselves on quick response time and strict quality control. They belong to arborist organizations throughout the country, so they are up on the latest information on treatments.
- *"These people have literally brought my lawn and bushes back to life. We live in an old home with lots of older plantings. The bushes were in sad condition and Tree Tech, over a period years, has worked hard to bring them back. They were 99% successful—we lost one azalea."*

✍ _____

Watchung Tree Service, (908)969-3215, UC MIC WC, 37 years in business

This tree service will provide its customers with trimming, topping, removals and stump removal. They can also make available for their customers firewood and woodchips.
- *"They have done a lot of work at our home over the years. When we first moved in , they removed two large pine trees. Every couple of years, we have them back to trim dead wood and branches. We also get our firewood from them."*

✍ _____

MASONS

Chico Mason Contractors Inc., (732)382-1676, MC SC WC, 8 years in business

Chico is willing to tackle any size job—large or small. He considers himself to be a perfectionist and so do his customers. His expertise is stonework.

- *"Good guy. He's a very good mason."*
- *"His stonework is excellent and he does his work on time."*
- *"I would highly recommend him to others."*

John Connelly Construction, (908)638-5450, MC SC, 25 years in business

Connelly Construction has a special technique which they use when installing stone. This gives the stone the appearance of always having been there. They also will install bluestone around patios and pools and have built waterfalls stone veneers.

- *"We have used him and he is fabulous."*
- *"He is a master stone mason who does the absolute finest, high-end quality work. His stonework is admired by everyone we know."*

Josantos Construction Inc., (973)589-1731, A, 19 years in business

This concrete mason/contractor specializes in pool decks, sidewalks, driveways and patios.

- *"My husband is extremely high on Joe and very impressed with his work."*
- *"He did a major renovation on a patio and it is absolutely beautiful. We have recommended him to our friends who have all thought he was great!"*

Ernest Novello & Son, (908)756-8291, UC SC, 38 years in business

Each of Novello & Son's jobs is a custom creation tailored to fit the clients' needs. Their masonry experience and expertise guarantee that the end result will be aesthetically pleasing.

- *". . . installed a patio 10 years ago and did a beautiful job."*
- *"I feel he is a supreme craftsman."*

Louis A. Nucci Construction, (973)377-8081, UC MC SC, 28 years in business

The masons that are employed by Louis Nucci have combined over 85 years of experience.

They specialize in masonry fireplaces, new construction, and repairing existing structures.
- *"After 17 years our front steps had to be replaced. He did a beautiful job of brick and slate. We were very satisfied with his work."*

✍ _____
_____
_____

A. Pigna & Son, (908)322-7382, A, 35 years in business

The employees of Pigna consider themselves artists not just masons. They enjoy working with all types of stone on walls, walkways, steps, etc.
- *"He constructed a beautiful brick wall that goes along my driveway. We were thrilled at how elegant it made our house look."*
- *"He has done masonry work for everyone in my neighborhood. We're all thrilled."*
- *"He did my front walk. Came when he said he would and completed the job on time. We were very happy!"*

✍ _____
_____
_____

Stonescape Construction, (973)560-0539, A, 15 years in business

Stonescape construction installs concrete pavers, retaining walls, drainage systems patios and walkways. They are certified by the ICPI (Interlocking Concrete Pavers Institute).
- *"They did our walkways and patio in our new home. It was an excellent job and they were very prompt."*
- *"They are gentlemen and they stand by their work. These people will return after all is settled to make sure the job is still perfect."*
- *"They do beautiful work. I enjoyed having them around and would highly recommend them."*

✍ _____
_____
_____

AIR & DUCT CLEANING

R & R Kleen Sweep, (973)526-1064, UC SC MC MIC, 14 years in business
Any duct cleaning including dryer vent cleaning is done by this company. They will also do cleaning and repairing of chimneys.
- *"They come on schedule and are very thorough. "*
- *"This can be a very messy job but they kept everything contained to one area. Great cleanup."*

Space Age Inc., (888)553-2624, A, 2 years in business
Space Age claims to make your home healthier and therefore a healthier you. Their professionals have combined their proven techniques with the patented Roto-Brush Duct Cleaning System. This cleaning method thoroughly scrubs and vacuums your ducts.
- *"They are very nice people to deal with. Very accommodating. They did a good job and cleaned up before they left without a trace."*

ANTIQUE FURNITURE AND COLLECTIBLES MOVER

Furniture Delivery by Bob, (908)735-8924, A, 20 years in business
This husband-and-wife team takes great care in moving antiques which have been purchased in an antique shop of comparable location. They have been moving furniture for 20 years with many satisfied customers.
- *"I have purchased at separate times a huge oak dresser and a very detailed antique china cupboard. Bob and Sally moved these pieces into my home with the utmost care."*
- *"As an antique dealer, we need someone dependable and meticulously careful in the transport of our furniture. We use Furniture Delivery and recommend them to our customers. Our customers are always pleased with their service."*

ANTIQUE FURNITURE RESTORATION

Davis & Eldridge Fine Antique Restoration, (201)252-8340, A, 25 years in business
Davis and Eldridge are in a class by themselves. They are one of the few who are knowledgeable and qualified to restore high-end period furniture, such as Federal and George III. They will do gold leafing, French polishing, and color matching. A custom reproduction manufacturing service is also available.

- *"He is just a great guy. I like him a lot, very knowledgeable. He will also build furniture."*
- *"They refinished our dining-room table with a French polish. It is just beautiful. The grain in the wood shows up and is so lovely. They even shined up the brass feet."*

ASBESTOS REMOVAL

Finishing Touch Asbestos Abatement Corp., (732)222-8372, A, 18 years in business
Finishing Touch has been in the asbestos remedial business for many years. They have completed asbestos projects for the U.S. Army, Air Force, Navy, Coast Guard, IRS, and hundreds of schools throughout New Jersey, New York and Pennsylvania. They specialize in residential abatement and inspections.
- *"This company removed asbestos from the heat pipes, water pipes and all sorts of pipes in our basement. Not a flake was left behind. Everything was washed down and was immaculate when they left."*

AWNINGS

F & S Awning and Blind Co. Inc., (732)738-5790, A, 17 years in business
Bob Trotte, owner of F & S Awning and Blind brings to the canvas awning business over 50 years of experience. He takes pride in his craft of manufacturing and installing fabric awnings for both residential and commercial purposes. They offer a unique take-down, storage and rehanging service.
- *"Very, very reliable. They routinely come out to us to clean our awnings. They also store our awnings."*
- *"They custom-made the awnings for our home and we have been using them for the past eight years."*

Laggren's Inc., (908)756-1948, A, 100 years in business
Any type of awning from plain to elaborate can be manufactured and installed by Laggren's. All awnings are custom-made and can be cotton, acrylic, vinyl or aluminum.
- *"They custom-made an awning for our outdoor porch. In the winter they will come and take it down, store it and redeliver for us. They have a convenient and very helpful service."*

L N Enterprises, (908)757-1819, A, 13 years in business
Awnings and canopy cleaning is the specialty of this family-owned-and-operated busi-

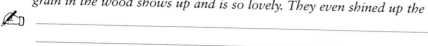

MISCELLANEOUS

ness. They pride themselves on being able to maintain a personal relationship with their customers. They treat their customers like they would like to be treated.

- *"They cleaned our awnings which truly turned out looking like they were brand new."*
- *"They are easy to work with and very nice."*

Maplewood Awning & Shade Co., (973)761-6565, A, 90 years in business
Fabric awnings, window shades and blinds are all manufactured by Maplewood.

- *"They measured all the windows in my in-law's home. The delivery and installation were right on target. A very nice job. They worked well with older people who really needed someone who knew what they were doing."*

BRASS POLISHING & REPAIR

The Brass Shop, (908)232-2161, A, 35 years in business
For 35 years this family has been taking care of brass and silver pieces. They will also do lamp repairs and new and antique lighting.

- *"They have shined many of my brass pieces from candlesticks to chandeliers and did a marvelous job."*
- *"They do great work. I have used them for years for my brass chandelier and sconces. He finishes exactly when he says he will."*

CABINET CONSTRUCTION

David Leiz Custom Woodworking Inc., (908) 486-1533, UC, 22 years in business
Any type of cabinet (wood or laminate) can be constructed by David Leiz. He has built vanities, kitchens, entertainment units, libraries and built-in bedrooms. He is a certified Corian Fabricator.

- *"We have a very large master bedroom and bathroom. David made all the cabinets and they are just wonderful. He is reliable and trustworthy and a genuine nice person. Several of my friends have used him for kitchen cabinets and were just as pleased."*

Michael's Custom Kitchen, (908)276-8991, A, 47 years in business
Michael, better known as Mickey, has the expertise of 47 years in the business of building media centers, wall units, bookcases, vanities and more. All are custom-designed ,

manufactured and installed. If you are thinking of renovating your kitchen he will also do kitchen cabinets.

- *"He made built-in cabinets on either side of the fireplace with furniture-quality cherry wood. He did a wonderful job. We found him very easy to get along with."*

CARPET INSTALLATION

Carpet Connection, (732)634-8329, A, 25 years in business
Ron Rosko of Carpet Connection will install and repair any carpet.

- *"He is so reliable and pleasant. His work is very good."*
- *"We installed tile in our foyer. When it was finished there was a gap between the tile and the wall-to-wall carpet from the living room. The tile man said I would probably have to live with it, but then I found Ron. He was able to fill in the gap with the existing rug."*

S.K. Hamrah Carpets, (908)756-8000, UC SC MIC, 63 years in business
Hamrah will install any carpet whether purchased there or somewhere else.

- *"They are reliable. Laid my carpets down in my home and did a fine job. They have been around for years."*

CHAIR CANING

The Caning Peg, (908)735-8924, A, 20 years in business
What started out as a hobby for this antique collector became a full-time job. It seems that everyone has a broken seat in need of repair. No job is too small and pick-up and delivery can be arranged.

- *"She does excellent work. Always kept to her schedule and delivers on time."*
- *"As an antique dealer it is difficult to find certain people for various restoring. Sally has done recaning of chairs and rushing. She is meticulous and completes to perfection."*

CLEANING SERVICES

Exclusively House Cleaning Inc., (908)233-2286, UC MC SC, 12 years in business
This house-cleaning service will come to your home either weekly, biweekly or for a

spring cleanup job. The customer is provided with a cleaning lady who takes pride in her job. Supervision is often provided to guarantee the highest quality service. They are fully insured and bonded.

- *"They are very professional and exceptionally trustworthy. The owner Marlene, really cares. They have a wonderful reputation."*

 _____

_____

Maid Brigade Services, (908)789-0700, UC MC SC MIC, 18 years in busines

This is a nationally franchised residential cleaning service that will offer the customer routine housecleaning, regular service and one-time service for move-in and move-out. Their employees are covered by Workman's Compensation, General Liability and Bonding Insurance. Uniformed and trained, they show up at your doorstep with all their own supplies and equipment.

- *"We have been using them for quite some time. They are always very careful with my possessions. They are dependable and honest (which means a lot when you are leaving someone in your home if you are at work)."*

 _____

_____

CUSTOM LAMPSHADE DESIGN

Williams Lamp Salon, (908)232-2158, UC, 60+ years in business

Williams will provide custom shades and replacement shades in all sizes and shapes using the customer's fabrics or their own. They have thousands of styles to choose from. They make string shades, crackle parchment, cutouts, silks, laminates and handpainted shades.

- *"The people at Williams have been wonderful in advising me on the choice of shades for a chandelier in my dining room. They sat down with me and we must have looked at hundreds of styles before we finally found one we liked. It was quite an unusual style—very Victorian—and when the shades were installed they looked great."*

_____

_____

CUSTOM SCREENING AND GLASS

Disco Aluminum, (908)754-2699, A, 15 years in business

Disco Aluminum is a manufacturer of screens and glass to size. They will do custom screening and porch enclosures. Custom repairs are also routinely done.

- *"One of the most special places in my home is our screened-in porch. Disco has kept my screens in excellent condition."*
- *"They are very careful to not damage the existing frames when replacing screens on my porch. They are great people to do business with."*

_____

_____

DECORATIVE PILLOWS

Feather Your Nest, (609)581-8223, A, 10+ years in business
The pillows designed by Janine Pettit are created to reflect the style and taste of the home-owner. She loves the challenge of recreating something someone has seen in a magazine or designing something new. Feather Your Nest was originally created by Janine's desire to make use of vintage fabrics. She had her own collection of antique needle- and petit-point that she used to create down-filled pillows. As time went on she began to salvage vintage damask cloths, antique lace and other materials. She works with all kinds of fabrics to turn people's ideas into reality and help customers create the look they want.

- *"Janine does beautiful work. I purchased from her four beautiful pieces of very old needlepoint and with the fabrics of my choice, she created the most beautiful pillows."*
- *"She has made some beautiful pillows for me and it didn't take forever. They were delivered to me when she said they would be."*
- *"She is the kind of person that I really am glad I had the opportunity to meet. Her pillows are such that one will always treasure them."*

_____
_____
_____

DOCK CONSTRUCTION

R.H. LeChard and Sons Inc., (732)892-0735, A, 71 years in business
This marine construction business will dredge, put in foundation piles, bulkheads and docks.

- *"They are very experienced. When we moved into our beachhouse the dock needed extensive repair. John was recommended to us and now we agree that he is truly 'the legend of the shore.'"*

_____
_____
_____

DRUM REPAIR

Drum Cellar, (908)685-9797, A, 3 years in business
Peter Mascola's business has been built on years of referrals. His helpfulness is extended to everyone in the areas of restoration, repairing, selling and refinishing drums. His honesty is often appreciated by parents of young children because they are not familiar with the levels of drums.

- *"The work that comes to my mind is honesty. He also does quality workmanship."*
- *"He can take a drum that is in bad shape and make it look like new."*

_____
_____
_____

MISCELLANEOUS

ENVIRONMENTAL CONSTRUCTION

Chatham Environmental & Construction Co., (973)635-8344, UC MC, 2 years in business
Chatham offers turnkey services ranging from paving, concrete construction, Belgian block, to underground storage tank services. They custom-tailor their services to provide customers with a professional, personal and cost-efficient solution. Their key field managers have collectively over 28-years experience in the environmental construction industry.
- *"They did our sidewalk which was very difficult. They did a very professional job and we have had no problems at all since the work was done. I would highly recommend him and definitely use him again."*

FINE GLASS/CRYSTAL RESTORATION

Art Cut Glass Studio Inc., (732)583-7648, A, 27 years in business
Fine glass restoration is a highly specialized skill. It is very hard to find people that have been highly trained and experienced in glass cutting, engraving and sculpting to restore something that has been damaged. Art Cut Glass will bring that treasured piece back to life.
- *"When you break an heirloom that has been in the family for years you think you want to die. I had broken a piece of Steuben that belonged to my grandmother. I took it to him and really was expecting him to say it could not be repaired. He didn't. He repaired it and you would not know it had been broken. He's wonderful."*
- *"I have a candelabra with figurines. He repaired it where it had chipped and no one would ever know it had been touched."*
- *"He's very honest and does a beautiful, beautiful job. I literally gave him my crystal piece in 'humpty-dumpty' pieces and he put it back together again."*

FIREPLACE ENCLOSURES

S.G. Installations, (908)735-6049, UC SC MIC WC, 14 years in business
Steve will come to the home to measure and install custom glass and screen enclosures for fireplaces.
- *"Knowing Steve for so many years has been a pleasure."*
- *"He is so willing to please and does a masterful job . He responds to phone calls immediately and his work is to perfection."*

FLAG AND FLAGPOLE INSTALLATION

Global Flag & Flagpole Supply Inc., (800)441-3524, A, 25 years in business

Global sells flags, banners, pennants and flagpoles. They will install, service and maintain all outdoor displays. Flags and banners are made using acid and fiber reactive dye, four-color process and surface ink-screen printing.

- *"They are pleasant and prompt."*
- *"I did not have my flagpole installed but my neighbor did. It was a difficult job, but these people were so pleasant. They told me they would maintain my flagpole. I think I'll take them up on it."*

GARAGE DOOR SALES AND SERVICE

Bridgewater Overhead Doors, (908)725-5655, SC WC, 27 years in business

Bridgewater Overhead Doors will install residential doors, commercial steel-rolling doors and garage-door openers. They provide 24-hour emergency service.

- *"They installed four garage doors with openers for us. We haven't had to use them for service for we have not had one problem since installation."*

Drozic Door Sales & Installations, (908)889-8850, A, 27 years in business

This company will do carpentry, sales, installation and repairs of garage doors and electric openers. They pride themselves on doing their own work and not subcontracting. Customers will always be called back within 24 hours and they try to do repairs in a reasonable time frame.

- *"Drozic installed two garage doors plus openers. They made everything so simple that it was a breeze."*
- *"He came when he said and installed really nice doors. It's a wonderful service and he's a good businessman."*

Metropolitan Door Company, (908)233-5836, A, 51 years in business

Established in 1946, Metropolitan Door has been serving the Central New Jersey area. They have consistently won for the last five years Raynor's Sales Achievement award making them Raynor's largest residential distributor in the tri-state area.

- *"They are prompt and reliable."*

Martin J. Metzger, (908)276-7607, UC MIC, 15 years in business

Marty Metzger's primary business is garage door and opener sales and installation and repairs. His only advertising is by word-of-mouth from other satisfied customers.

MISCELLANEOUS

• *"He installed our garage door openers. We were absolutely lost without openers and he suggested a certain brand that worked perfectly. It's a real safety issue in my mind—now I don't have to get out of my car in the dark driveway to open the garage door."*

GARDEN PHOTOGRAPHY

Karl W. Faller Photography, (617)235-7014, A, 26 years in business
Karl Faller has been a fine art photographer for over 26 years. He specializes in large format photography, landscape and gardens. Portfolio is available via mail on request.

• *"He takes absolutely magnificent beautiful photos. He did a series of lady slipper & wild phlox photos over a lapse of time and framed them in a long narrow frame. His work is truly a treasure."*

GAS GRILL INSTALLATION

S.G. Installations, (908)735-6049, UC SC MIC WC, 10 years in business
Steve offers, in addition to installations a complete rebuilding service which includes stripping and repainting. He will test for gas leaks and pressure and check the groundpost. He specializes in replacing hard-to-find parts in older gas grills with exact manufacturers' parts. Steve will also convert grills from propane to natural gas.

• *"He installed our gas grill. We thought we would have a hard time finding someone to do it because we brought it with us from our old home. He was a godsend . . . did the job beautifully. No muss, no fuss. A really nice guy."*

GAS LOG INSTALLATION

S.G. Installations, (908)735-6049, UC SC MIC WC, 10 years in business
Steve has 10 years of experience installing gas logs and fireplace accessories. He has extensive knowledge of fireplace installations and repairs. He deals with all manufacturers and models and evening appointments are available.

• *"Steve services our gas fireplaces. He is a true treasure. He's very careful in my home and is meticulously clean—which is a plus when cleaning and installing anything around a fireplace."*
• *"He is agreeable to work with and is flexible with scheduling. He's very responsive to phone calls."*

GRANITE FABRICATION

Amalfi Marble, (908)272-8844, A, 14 years in business
Amalfi Marble specializes in restoring, polishing, grinding, sealing, grout cleaning, stone enhancing and repairs of marble, granite, limestone and terra-cotta. They will also clean and polish scratched or stained marble.

- *"They reground and refinished marble and terrazzo floors in our home which were 30 years old. When they were finished and polished, they looked better than original. I was really thinking of ripping the floors up but I'm glad I didn't.*

Renaissance Marble and Granite Inc., (609)227-3535, A, 9 years in business
This is a full-service marble and granite fabricator. They will custom-cut and polish kitchen counters, bath suites, fireplaces and more. Services include templating, stone selection assistance and fabrication installation.

- *"They are very good, very nice. They did our granite countertops in the kitchen. We also had marble tops installed in a bathroom. They did two marble fireplace hearths with beveled edges. The edges are beautifully rounded and polished perfectly."*
- *"When we completely reconstructed our house, many of the contractors were a horror and I could not recommend them for this book. However, Renaissance was wonderful and I would highly recommend them!"*

Statewide Granite & Marble Inc., (201)653-1700, A, 12 years in business
Statewide offers a full service of fabrication and installation for countertops, stairs, tub surrounds, fireplaces and tables. Keeping the quality high is their main objective. They have a well-equipped factory with modern state-of-the-art machinery.

- *"Excellent for fabricating that I actually purchased elsewhere. They were very helpful in selecting the best edge for a table. They did an excellent job."*

HOUSE MEDIA INSTALLATION

Diversified Installations, (908)850-5400, A, 13 years in business
This company provides unique and exclusive services to the homeowner. Decisions need to be made in wiring the home and installation of built-in systems. They take the time to determine the client's needs so that the end product will be a system built around specific lifestyle.

- *"They are very good. They wired our home for television, cable stereo, CD player and alarm system. They have fabulous workers."*
- *"They are very knowledgeable as to the state-of-the-art equipment which was especially nice since we hadn't a clue."*

Stuarts Audio-Video, (908)232-0483, A, 40 years in business

If you have thought of: music distributed to each room, home theater wiring, video distributed to each room, cable, satellite, antenna wiring for the future, a telephone system that can be used as an intercom, doorbells that ring through phones, cameras at every entrance, lighting control automated as part of the security system and more—all are possible if the wiring is incorporated into the initial design of the house. At Stuarts they sit down with the customer and design a plan for the proper wiring based upon industry standards to future-proof your home.

- *"Stuarts did prewiring during our construction phase. We found them extremely helpful. They worked with the plans for the layout as to where the speakers would go."*
- *"They designed a unit for our television that drops out of the ceiling so the TV takes up no room in our living room."*
- *"Excellent service. They always know exactly what to do. We have purchased all of our TV and audio equipment from them."*

INDOOR AND OUTDOOR HOLIDAY DECORATIONS

Benninger Sons, (908)232-8084, UC, 15 years in business

Beninger Sons can provide that special touch for outside Christmas displays. They will hang outdoor lights or wreaths.

- *"They strung lights on an old, huge pine tree in my yard that for years was crying to be decorated. We had thought that the job was too difficult, but they did it with ease and now every Christmas that tree looks very impressive."*

Ferguson & McQuillan, (908)791-1224, UC MC SC MIC, 3 years in business

People have such a hectic schedule at Christmastime and it can be very difficult to find the time to decorate the home. Ferguson & McQuillan help take this worry away. They make their own decorations in their workshop and will happily bring them to your home and do all the decorating themselves. Their materials are fresh or dried and they can work with a mixture of both if desired. They specialize in interior home decorating but will do minor "hang-ups" on the outside. Make sure you call them well in advance.

- *"They did my front hall. Provided a garland on the banister and a beautiful garland on a huge window in my dining room. Everything looked fabulous and I know that I could not have done it as well by myself."*
- *"They provide the most interesting mixture of fresh and dried materials in their arrangements. They are truly creative."*

Scarlet Begonias, (908)654-9735, A, 3 years in business

For that very tall pine tree that just must have lights on it, or that hard to reach spot to put a wreath, these are the people to call. They will also completely take over the creation of your outdoor lighting/decorating scheme.

- *"They decorated the outside of my home at Christmas. They hung wreaths in high windows. I purchased the wreaths and lovely bows from them and everything looked beautiful."*
- *"Samantha had the most beautiful garland and she very artistically draped it over an outside railing and on some cement structures. So creative. They are truly the nicest people to work with."*

IN-HOME RUG AND CARPET SALES

Shehadi Rugs & Carpet, (973)635-8100, A, 23 years in business
Shehadi Rugs & Carpet is very fortunate to have on their staff Barbara Kitson, designer, who will come to your home for consultation on Oriental rugs. She will also provide samples of broadlooms. She makes every effort to give her customers excellent service from start to finish.

- *"I have known Barbara for many years. She knows the rug business like the back of her hand. Barbara has offered me many opinions on our Oriental rugs."*
- *"This is a person who will go out of her way to fit you into her schedule. When you meet Barbara you immediately feel confident in her knowledge."*

INTERIOR HOME PORTRAITS

Brian Townsend, (908)756-1707A, 10 years in business
Brian will come to the home and consult with the owner on room decor, lighting and placement before he does a rough sketch. The customer can then make desired changes from the drawings. His portraits are done in oil on canvas and to the size desired by his clients.

- *"This was truly one of the most precious things in my home. We had asked Brian to do a painting of our entry hall after having seen some of his work. The painting is absolutely beautiful and he has captured the beautiful architectural work in our hallway. It hangs in a prominent place in our house and I know it is something I will treasure forever."*
- *"We asked Brian to do a painting of our library. This is truly one of the most charming rooms in our house and he definitely captured the feeling on canvas. He is truly a wonderful artist."*

LAMP REPAIR

Williams Lamp Salon, (908)232-2158, UC, 60 years in business
Williams makes just about anything into a lamp. They enjoy a challenge and will restore

old lamps, refinish and rewire. Many of their lamps have been published and the founder Evan T. Williams has had many patents in the lamp industry.

- *"We go back about 18 years. We have always brought all our lamp repairs to Williams. They are honest business people and I will continue to use them."*

LOCK AND SAFE INSTALLATION

Bill's Lock, Safe & Security, (908)241-0203, A, 15 years in business
We thought it was significant that last month Bill Kushnick finished fifth in the world in Lockmasters' International Safe Lock Manipulation Contest. He has an impressive background—a graduate of NJIT in Engineering and he had opened safes on TV. He is a contributing author for *Safe and Vault Technology* magazine.

- *"Bill installed an in-ground safe in our basement. He is so knowledgeable and he's meticulous. I felt very comfortable with him."*
- *"He installed dead-bolt locks for us. We were so pleased that we recommended him to our friends and they were pleased too."*

MARBLE FLOOR CLEANING

Paragon Maintenance Inc., (908)470-9036, A, 25 years in business
Paragon's specialty is complete marble restoration. They will also supply the homeowner with complete maintenance and restoration of hard floors such as granite, slate and ceramic tile.

- *"Vinnie is my marble man. He performs miracles with marble. We had an incontinent dog who made a total mess of our marble floor as she aged. After we put her to sleep, we called Vinnie and he repolished the marble and lifted out every stain. The floor is now like brand-new."*
- *"He has done a lot of polishing for us. I have never used anyone else. Always punctual."*

MODEL SHIPS AND YACHTS

Historic Model Ships and Yachts, (732)681-3276, A, 30 years in business
Mr. William Magara restores and custom-builds ship models, which duplicate legendary vessels in precise scaled-down detail. He strives for realism of construction, appearance and authenticity. Models are constructed in the same way full-sized counterparts were built, hull-framed and planked with functional rigging. To achieve these goals, he spends considerable time on research and planning for each ship to be constructed.

- *"He made two glass cases for antique model ships for me. They were beautifully constructed."*
- *"I have seen models he has constructed and it's amazing the amount of work and talent that is involved. They are truly works of art."*

✍ _____
_____
_____

MUSICAL INSTRUMENT REPAIR

David A. Bierman Band Instrument Repair, (908)322-8356, A, 5 years in business
David repairs wind-type and brass-band instruments. Having started out as a music teacher, David knows what it's like to wait several weeks for an instrument to be repaired. Hence his service is very quick.
- *"He was recommended by a friend. He must have a wonderful word-of-mouth business."*
- *"He is dependable, efficient. He repaired an old flute for us."*

✍ _____
_____
_____

Ira B. Kraemer & Co., (908)322-4469, A, 30 years in business
Ira Kraemer repairs, restores and will appraise stringed instruments such as rare violins, violas, cellos and bows. He does consultation by special arrangement in the home.
- *"A man with great integrity. He is a true craftsman."*
- *"You can hold up an instrument for him and he can immediately tell you the age, where it was made, etc. He's incredible."*

✍ _____
_____
_____

OIL PAINTING RESTORATION

Swain Galleries, (908)756-1707, A, 129 years in business
Oil paintings that have been punctured, need cleaning, revarnishing or relining, or are badly flaked can be restored by Swain. In fact, most restoration problems can be solved by this regional institution. Pick-up and delivery are offered.
- *"We had a painting that had been in my family for years. It was a portrait of a very unattractive lady and she needed restoration desperately. Swain picked her up, relined the canvas, touched up where necessary and delivered and hung my lady. Even though she's truly an ugly woman, the painting looks beautiful."*

✍ _____
_____
_____

OIL TANK REMOVAL

A-1 Tank Cleaning Service, (973)736-5020, A, 20 years in business

As experienced oil-burner servicemen, the owners of this company are aware and capable of servicing oil tank problems. Their services include tank cleaning, tank removal and tank installation.

- *"My neighbors recommended them to us. The job was well-done and they are very reliable."*

Top Grade Inc., (908)903-1300, A, 7 years in business

Top Grade offers a full line of environmental services including: tank closure, tank testing, above and underground tank installations, tank location, tank cleaning, and soil remediation. People who are faced with concerns about an underground tank will find that this company has a goal to ease any worries in a professional and economically advantageous manner.

- *"They were recommended to us by a neighbor. They removed our oil tank and did a good job. At that time we had contaminated soil. They took soil samples on the same day and arranged to have the soil disposed."*
- *"They are extremely professional and did a wonderful job removing our oil tank. It was a messy job but they're the ones to do it."*

OUTDOOR FURNITURE RE-STRAPPING

Angel's Restrapping, (973)942-9681, A, 17 years in business

Why wait until your patio furniture falls apart? Angel's will repair, restrap or refinish aluminum outdoor patio furniture and patio umbrellas. They specialize in Molla Medallion and most top manufacturers and provide pick-up and delivery.

- *"I have Brown Jordan–strapped furniture. My dog chewed up the chaise. It was very difficult to find someone but eventually someone recommended Angel to me. He is very pleasant and ordered the necessary material to restrap the chair. He did a beautiful job."*
- *"He provides pick-up and delivery and is easy to work with. Believe me me this is such a specialty that it is hard to find someone to do it. I hope this recommendation is helpful to people."*

OUTSIDE STRUCTURES

Florham Park Hardware, (973)377-3121, UC MC, 20 years in business

After a customer selects and orders one of their storage buildings, Florham Park conducts an on-site inspection of the premises before delivering. They will review placement of the structure and color compatability and coordinate with the customer. They lay out the four corners of the building with strings so that the customer may visualize this before installation.

- *"He's the best in the business. He installed a shed in our backyard. He was on time and reliable. A personable guy, a perfect job. We love and use the shed."*

PAPER AND PRINT RESTORATION

Martayan Lan, (800)423-3741, A, 15 years in business
This company specializes in the restoration of antique maps and rare books.

- *"I am a collector of old maps. They have done restoration for me. They are world class in their field . . . very conscientious. I believe they are considered in the handful of the best. They have a worldwide clientele."*

Swain Galleries, (908)756-1707, A, 129 years in business
Swain will clean and deacidify works on paper. They will also repair and fill paper as needed.

- *"We found beautiful, old etchings in the attic of my grandmother's house. They had been affected by the moisture and had terrible mildew stains. Swain came to the house, got rid of the stains and restored them, and redelivered and hung them. I love they way they look now."*

RAILINGS

Cusumano Perma Rail Company, (908)245-9281, UC, 35 years in business
This company fabricates custom-wrought iron and aluminum railings, window guards and gates. All customers have an opportunity to choose their own designs and style.

- *"They measured and installed custom-wrought iron railings for our basement windows. I was concerned about it being too easy for someone to get into my home. Never a problem with the work, and the railings were attractive to the eye."*

Nick's Railing, Inc., (908)241-1006, A, 25 years in business
Nick Patella designs and fabricates ornamental ironworks from either wrought iron or aluminum.

- *"I designed the railings that were to go in the front of our home. He was very cooperative in helping me with the design. When one of the railings was complete he called me so I could look at it before he installed it. The finished railings are perfect."*

- *"A very competent craftsman. Easy to work with and quick to respond to my phone calls. I hope since I recommended him that he would want to be in the book because he's a really nice guy and does a great job."*

SEWER AND DRAIN CLEANING

Coventry & Froehlich Sewer & Drain Cleaning, (908)276-3550, UC, 17 years in business
Do you have clogged sewers or drains? Coventry & Froelich will be there to clean them.
- *"They have come to our home more than once to snake our bathtub. They're very responsive and come quickly. They clean up well."*

Macaulay's Sewer Service, Inc., (800)843-1741, A, 5 years in business
Everybody at one time or another has needed a Macaulay's. They specialize in cleaning clogged sewers and drains. Extended warranties are offered to ease customers' minds.
- *"They cleaned our drains two times. We were happy with his job."*
- *"We decided to use him after I got tired of bugging my husband to attend to the job. I was so glad I called him. They did a great job. They are conscientious, come quickly and I must say he loves his work."*

SILVER CLEANING AND PLATING

Bermel Quality Plating Inc., (973)674-2711, A, 50 years in business
Bermel can bring your old antiques back to life. They do gold and silver plating and metal refinishing on holloware, tea services, brass, copper, white metal and church pieces.
- *"We inherited some silver items from my husband's family. They were in terrible shape. They made them look like new. They did a great job."*
- *"They replated a large platter. I thought there was no hope for it but they did an outstanding job. I was more than satisfied."*
- *"They made pieces which looked 'junky' to me look like they just came out of Tiffany's, Cartier or the jeweler of your choice."*

Sterling Silversmith, (908)322-5854, A, 49 years in business

Silverplating, refinishing, repairing and restoration of silver and pewter have all been done for close to fifty years by this business—by father, then son. Tony will be happy to make "house calls" for insurance appraisal or to give an estimate for cleaning.

- *"He soddered a handle on a piece of silver and it has never come off again."*
- *"He is very helpful. I had an old lamp that needed to be replated. I brought it to several places and they wouldn't do it for it was a small job. Then I found Tony. He did a beautiful job."*
- *"He has done a great job polishing odds and ends of silver pieces that have been in my family for years."*

SNOWPLOWING

Bravo Landscape Construction, (908)322-4678, UC, 11 years in business

Bravo really cares about the customer's property. They pride themselves on reliability.

- *"They do a superb job. Every snowflake is gone."*
- *"We have been using him for several years and he is very dependable."*

Joseph's Landscaping, (973)644-3443, MC, 5 years in business

This snow removal company cares about the customer being able to safely exit from their home after a snowfall. They take special care to avoid lawn damage.

- *"He is the hardest worker I know. A terrific guy."*
- *"Very, very reliable."*

Antonino Pafumi Contractor, (908)232-4236, UC, 37 years in business

Snowplowing is done for commercial and residential properties. Full service includes: salting, sanding, snow removal, loader and dumptruck services.

- *"The Pafumis have been plowing our property for years. They have never let us down . . . are always there when we need them."*
- *"I admire them for they pride themselves on their dependability and they truly can be counted on to do a great job."*

Rosa Snowplowing, (732)388-5801, UC SC MIC, 5 years in business

For five years Mike Rosa has plowed people out in the worst of snowstorms. He prides himself on being dependable for his customers.

- *"You can always count on him. He has been plowing our driveway since he first started out."*

- *"It's a comfortable feeling when you see the first snowflake and know when you wake in the morning there will be no problem getting to work."*

_____
_____

Westfield Landscaping, (908)232-4094, UC, 14 years in business

With a personal and dependable service established for over a decade, Jimmy will plow your driveways with the utmost care.

- *"Jimmy has been doing our plowing for several years. We have three driveways oddly situated and he does an excellent job. He is very careful to not destroy the edges of the lawn."*
- *"Exceptionally dependable."*

_____
_____

STONECARVER

Gabriele Hiltl-Cohen, (609)448-8375, A, 12 years in business

Gabriele has done interior and exterior stonecarving for architects, landscape architects, contractors and private patrons. Her carvings include figures, foliage reliefs, cornices, capitals, architectural moldings and lettering. She has also carved gargoyles, fountains and garden sculpture. Restoration of existing sculptures is also offered. Work is done in natural stone such as: marble, granite limestone, sandstone, bluestone and slate. However, she is not restricted to stone. Many of her pieces are part of private collections in both the U.S. and Germany.

- *"I have seen a few of her carvings and I just had to recommend her for this book. They are so unique and effective. We are reconfiguring our garden and we plan on commissioning her to do a carving for us."*

_____
_____

VACUUM CLEANER REPAIR

Electrolux, (800)544-4098, UC SC WC, 13 years in business

Steve Cichowski knows the best equipment to address each customer's cleaning needs. Personal attention is given to each customer and pick-up and delivery of any repair job is free. Customers are his best source of advertising so therefore they receive 200% of his attention.

- *"Steve has been servicing my vacuum for many years. He will even deliver vacuum bags when needed."*
- *"He responds to his phone calls more than immediately. Most of the time he is able to repair my vacuum in my home without taking it."*

_____

Gemvac, (908)755-1600, A, 45 years in business

This is an old-fashioned business which boasts about their honesty and fairness. They work with the customer to establish their needs and try to fix unusual problems with vacuum cleaners. They will go out of their way to order hard to get items.

- *"I bought my first vacuum cleaner without doing any research and it was a piece of junk. The motor failed within two years. Rather than buy a new one, they rebuilt the motor. Since then I have had several more repairs done and it is now working perfectly, thanks to Gemvac."*

The Eardly T. Petersen Co., Inc., (908)232-5723, A, 41 years in business

When the vacuum cleaner breaks, most people want fast, efficient service. Eardly Petersen can provide that service. They will pick up your "sick" vacuum cleaner and give it TLC. You will receive it back in a reasonable amount of time.

- *"They provide a good service. Very helpful and timely."*

WATER FILTRATION AND PURIFICATION

Culligan Water Conditioning, (800)272-0079, A, 60 years in business

With the continuing concerns about our environment, the need for a constant source of quality water in the future is becoming increasingly important. Culligan is ready to provide that source. Their in-house laboratory is on the leading-edge of high-tech water treatment. They will provide in-house water treatment and bottled water.

- *"We have been pleased with their service. We have used them for five years and they always deliver on time."*
- *"We have their drinking filtration system and find the water to be wonderful, chemical-free and clear."*

The Portasoft Company Inc., (908)233-4300, A, 52 years in business

Since 1945 this company has been helping homeowners control and improve the quality of water they use. They have pioneered in the development of more efficient water treatment eauipment. Their products cover a wide range of needs from small purification units for home use to large units used in industrial settings. Whatever your water problem, Portasoft has the answer.

- *"This company is a pleasure to deal with. They are extremely helpful."*
- *"We have used them for five years and never had a problem with the water softener or their service."*

MISCELLANEOUS

WATERPROOFING

Gregory Waterproofing Company Inc., (732)381-7928, UC SC MIC, 42 years in business
The crew from Gregory is highly experienced. They state in their literature that trying to stop water under pressure is an impossible task that will only work temporarily. Their three- step system does not stop water, but rather keeps it under control and gives it a place to go. They guarantee the areas of a basement they waterproofed for 10 years.
- *"He's great. They waterproofed our entire basement. They were efficient, timely and we have not had a problem since."*
- *"I am very fussy about neatness and cleanliness and they were just perfect for my house. When they were finished with the job, the edges were perfect and it looked like a professional cement job. To perfection."*

WATER SYSTEMS SPECIALIST

Summit Well & Pump Co. Inc., (732)356-2700, A, 30 years in business
The job of drilling a new well, installing a pump, or servicing an older well should be done by a professional such as Summit Well & Pump. This family-owned company has been serving the area for many years and they not only know where water is most likely to be found, but also the best method to employ to get it.If you want a new water-well drilled, need repairs on an old one or have a pump that needs service these are the people to call.
- *"When we purchased our home we inherited a well. They come every year to service and prime. They test the water and the pressure. They really know what they are doing."*
- *"Our pump broke down and they dug to remove and replace a new pump. They have great response time. We have used them for over 20 years."*

WINDOW TREATMENT INSTALLATION

B & B Decorator Service, (732)381-7709, A, 29 years in business
Window treatments, shades, blinds, verticals and minis can all be installed by Sam Goldberg. He prides himself on his prompt service.
- *"He has done mostly shades and miniblinds in my home. He returns calls immediately which I really like."*
- *"He has repaired treatments for me that he never installed. He's always very willing to help out. No job is too small for him."*

Ed Della Fera Custom Window Treatments, (732)901-6664, A, 13 years in business

Ed is an expert in the installation of draperies and window coverings. He will also resteam and repleat draperies. Expert measuring is also a plus. Ed is equipped to provide the customer with shades, blinds, shutters and verticals.

- *"Very meticulous and always on time with his appointments. He returns calls immediately."*
- *"He is efficient and an expert in his field. We have used him for eight years and he is so easy to work with. He's also knowledgeable."*
- *"I am constantly changing things in my home and Ed is constantly here making those changes. His window treatment installations are done to perfection plus you could never meet a nicer guy."*

WINE APPRAISER

Abigail Hartmann Associates, (212)316-5406, A, 12 years in business

Gayle Skluzacek of Abigail Hartmann will tell you that she developed the Appraisers Association test for wine appraising. She was the first to receive certification in this field. She will come to the customer's home and review your collection, identify and recommend conservation and storage techniques, and provide an objective report that has been carefully researched and documented to reflect current market value. Appraisals are offered for the purposes of estate, gift tax, charitable contribution, insurance, damage/loss, equitable distribution and resale.

- *"Gayle is so knowledgeable about wines. She also does a very thorough appraisal which will stand up to any scrutiny."*

WINE CELLAR CONSTRUCTION

New England Wine Cellars, (800)863-4851, A, 5 years in business

Fred Tregaskis has a strong design background and is a wine reviewer. With this love of wine and fine woodworking skills, he can offer the customer quality construction including wine storage, cooling, humidity control and design.

- *"We love our wine cellar. For years my husband kept his wine in a helter-skelter way. It was not good for the wine or us. Fred built a beautiful cellar and was able to utilize space that was perfect. We have even considered entertaining in the wine cellar—it's that nice."*

B D Movers Inc., (800)310-0912, A, 9 years in business

Recently a customer said to the owner of B D: "Your men are as strong as ox and walk like deer." He was talking about the skill and care of the employees of this company. Their philosophy is that people move an average of every four to five years and they want to move the same people every time, not just once. They are very proud of the fact that most of their moves come from referrals.

- *"They are excellent—extremely careful. They were recommended to me by a very particular friend and I figured if she recommended them they must be perfect."*

Chatham Moving & Storage, (973)635-7100, UC MC SC, 92 years in business

The full-time staff at Chatham Moving will relocate your entire household. They will also move antiques. All employees are salaried as opposed to being paid on commission.

- *"They did an excellent job of moving the entire contents of our home. We were very pleased with their service."*
- *"We found them to be very careful and very courteous."*

Lincoln Storage Warehouses, (800)242-5825, A, 110 years in business

Residential, commercial and international moves are handled by these movers. A particular area of interest is older-adult relocations including distribution of possessions to family members and sale of items not being moved through affiliated auction galleries.

- *"They moved us locally. They're honest, clean, reliable, dependable. They worked efficiently and were polite to me and my family."*
- *"When they moved us there was not a dent or nick or scratch on any of our possessions. They far exceeded our expectations. A job well-done."*

Simonik Moving & Storage, (800)526-4268, A, 20 years in business

Simonik is an agent for Allied Van Lines and they were awarded with the Allied Award of Excellence. They specialize in local, long-distance, household-office and commercial relocations.

- *"They handled our last move. I can't add enough superlatives. They were extremely careful of my favorite possessions as well as my not-so-favorite."*
- *"They were polite, quiet and very, very efficient. Everything arrived at our new house in perfect condition. For a move it was fairly painless."*

Sisser Brothers Inc., (908)756-3100, A, 84 years in business

For moving and packing, whether it be local, cross-country or international, Sisser has the experience and know-how. Since 1913, they have been moving thousands of satisfied customers.

- *"Any time we have ever moved in our lives I can always remember it was Sisser. When I married and through the years, we have also made several moves, and we have always used Sisser. So I can remember them as a child and an adult."*
- *"They are timely, efficient and dependable."*

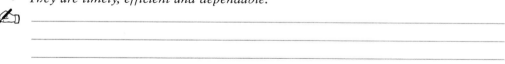

University Van Lines, (908)276-2070, UC MIC, 22 years in business

University will move you next door or to an international location. Customers include residential, offices and industrial.

- *"Oh, they were great. They were recommended to us by 'word-of-mouth' and the guys were very polite and personable. They were very careful with my belongings—there was no breakage. They were on time and we were thrilled with them."*
- *"For everything a mover should be, they were. I would definitely use them again. I know that my daughter and my sister will be using them in the near future."*

J.K. Vreeland Moving & Storage Co., (908)753-6515, A, 40 years in business

Vreeland specializes in executive relocations both local and long distance. This is a third-generation family-owned business and their employees take personal pride in their work. The owners take pride in the work their employees do.

- *"We used them for our last move and they made it absolutely painless."*
- *"They took great care during our move to pack all our valuables to prevent breakage and damage. Everything arrived at our new home the way we sent it."*
- *"Great crew."*

MUSICIANS

Block & Gerber Music and Entertainment, (800)255-4727, A, 14 years in business

Block & Gerber will customize party packages to suit the client's needs. They have been wedding specialists since 1983 and can accommodate any size party from 1 to 5000. They have entertained everyone from Queen Elizabeth, Charles and Diana, The N.Y. Mets '86 victory party and the President of the United States.

- *"He's terrific. He did our New Year's Eve party last year. A great entertainer and he has an enormous amount of energy."*
- *"He is just a wonderful piano player. He can play anything. In addition he's very entertaining and has the most engaging personality. He can be the life of the party and is a very talented musician."*

De Ja Vu Disc Jockeys, (908)722-1038, A, 9 years in business

Giving the customer exactly what they want for any occasion is the objective of these DJs. They believe that the customer is the best expert on their party and should choose the type of music they want. They will however give the customer advice based on their experience.

- *"Their DJs are good."*
- *"They are very entertaining. They do things to activate the crowd."*
- *"They have current music. People danced all night at our party."*

Janet Fitterer, (908)245-4731, UC MC, 15 years in business

Janet has provided piano music for any occasion for the past 15 years. She can offer music for your enjoyment—everything from the 20's to the 90's. For groups of people that really want to get into the party, Janet will provide sing-along cards for extra entertainment.

- *"A vivacious, dynamic person who will perform a variety of music in your home for a party."*
- *"She is out-of-this-world."*

G-Tech Entertainment, (908)353-3656, A, 20 years in business

G-Tech offers a wide range of musical styles from swing/standards of the 40's, Motown soul to contemporary dance/rock music. Groups are available from a three-piece soft-jazz piano trio up to a nine-piece dance band with full horn section They will tailor to any event.

- *"They play all types of music. Very accomplished musicians."*
- *"Great—a terrific band. They played at our wedding and people raved about them for months afterwards."*

Gig Line Entertainment, (908)630-0330, A, 5 years in business

This professional music company is managed by musicians who definitely know the business. They will do pre-party consultations and have actively performed in the tri-state area, finest concert halls and on Broadway. Every type of music is offered from classical to jazz, rock and rhythm and blues.

- *"He does private home parties providing really different kinds of music."*
- *"He's terrific. Very pleasant to work with. We used him for our daughter's wedding."*

Kueter & Mochernuk Piano Duo, (908)754-4442, A, 30 years in business

Piano music for parties, weddings, receptions and more is provided by Kueter & Mochernuk. They pride themselves on their musical flexibility and adaptability. They will play anything from light classical to popular music or soft jazz. Duet performances include special unique four-hand musical arrangements.

- *"Paul and his wife played at a party we had. They were absolutely wonderful. They played any type of music requested. My husband and I both enjoy listening to the piano and these two people were extraordinarily good."*
- *"They really know how to please the group. They are as professional as you can get."*

Ralph Mitchell Orchestras, (908)964-9196, A, 8 years in business

Ralph Mitchell offers musical entertainment for private parties, weddings and corporate events. Personal attention is given to individual needs.

- *"These are top-flight musicians. Truly professional."*
- *"We have attended two parties and they were both huge successes because of the music they provided."*

New Dimensions in Music, (908)233-9094, A, 40 years in business

Carolyn Klinger-Kueter is often called "the life of the party." She will play the accordion for any occasion and is often credited with getting the party going. Folk tunes, sing-alongs or background music are offered in her repertoire.

- *"She's a very upbeat person with a fabulous personality. She can definitely be an asset—I've seen her in action."*
- *"Extremely reliable. I'm so glad that I had the chance to meet her. She's a talented musician."*

Alan Quinn Orchestras, (201)823-4317, A, 15 years in business

Alan Quinn Orchestras have performed at countless concerts, corporate events, weddings, and private parties for 15 years. Their venues have included everything from Radio

City Music Hall and the United Nations to the Brooklyn Museum. Alan leads the band on piano and trumpet. His solo career includes performances with such noted acts as Dionne Warwick and Burt Bacharach, Donna Summer and the Jimmy Dorsey Big Band.

- *"An Alan Quinn Orchestra played at my friend's daughter's wedding. They were fabulous. You know how the band is so important at weddings. This band really got people dancing like crazy. I understand they also do parties in the home and I will definitely use them."*

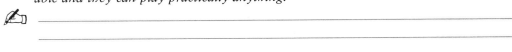

Summit Strings, (908)757-8905, UC MC SC MIC, 13 years in business

This group is experienced in selecting appropriate music for weddings or for anyone who wishes a string trio or quartet. They also can provide flute, trumpet, piano and vocalist. A large repertoire of classical and popular music is available and they can arrange musical requests that are not in their repertoire.

- *"We attended an at-home cocktail party. This group provided the jazz music. Everyone at the party at one point or another stopped to listen—they were that good! I would love to use them when I have my next party."*
- *"These people are so nice. Very easy to work with. I found them to be knowledgeable and they can play practically anything."*

PAINTERS

Ace Painting and Wallpaper, (908)879-7987, MC SC, 12 years in business
Whether it's brush, roller or spray, Ace Painting provides professional interior and exterior paint contracting work. Their ability to do faux painting, marbleizing and stenciling shows how versatile they are. Complete cleanup of the work area is an important part of their quality service.
- *"Being in the hardware business, I refer various tradespeople to my customers. I've referred Ace to many of my customers with good results."*
- *"They can handle any size job without any problems."*

Allen Painting, (908)879-9579, UC MC, 1 year in business
This is a young business with a young, ambitious crew eager to grow. They are very concerned about quality of work and aim to please by providing wonderful service.
- *"They showed up on time. Painted the inside walls and trim of the house. They were neat and clean and I would not hesitate to have him again."*

A.M. Painting & Papering, (908)638-4044, A, 10 years in business
A.M. does all three—interior painting, exterior painting and wallpaper hanging. Preparation and restoration of walls, ceilings, and trim are an area of concentration. Plastering and spackling are done to perfection. They pride themselves on having a professional crew and strive hard to complete the job to the customer's satisfaction.
- *"Very, very fine workers. They painted my downstairs and it was a huge job. Very high ceilings. They worked very hard. I hardly knew they were in the house."*
- *"Great painters."*

Celiz General Painting, (973)984-8904, A, 8 years in business
Hugo Celiz provides both interior and exterior painting. They have the ability to do power washing and electrical sanding. Complete house repair is also an option for homeowners using this firm.
- *"He is fantastic. We employed him after extensive review of the alternatives. He painted the outside of our big, old house and did a beautiful job."*
- *"I have recommended him to many people in my neighborhood."*

Custom Wallpaper & Painting, (973)669-8886, A, 15 years in business
This small business specializes in all types of wallcovering including designer and custom papers such as silk. They will also do painting including decorative and faux finishes.

- *"They are always on time. The nice thing about them is that they are creative enough to suggest extra touches when wallpapering."*

"Doctor" Jim's Home Repair Service, (908)273-8398, UC MC, 7 years in business

"Doctor" Jim's Home Repair provides interior and exterior painting and does light carpentry and odd jobs. No house call is too small for the Doctor!

- *". . . very organized, neat and punctual."*
- *"The absence of nothing bad made him good."*

Eloides Garcia Painting and Decorating, (908)233-7469, A, 22 years in business

Eloides Garcia is an interior and exterior painter. He also does exterior staining and will hang wallpaper.

- *"He's very professional, knows his products well."*
- *"He's very knowledgeable about painting techniques and will offer his own suggestions which are often very good."*

Gary's Home Improvement & Painting Co., (908)232-3557, A, 30 years in business

Gary has a professional and courteous staff that strives to satisfy the customer's painting needs (interior and exterior). He will also hang wallpaper.

- *". . . power washed and painted the outside of my home about five years ago. It has been holding up and we have had no great problems. The staff is courteous and speedy. They're nice people."*

George's A to Z Wallpapering, (908)232-6075, UC SC MIC W, 30 years in business

George's A to Z is a two-person operation specializing in interior's light painting and wallpapering. They work with the customer to do all or part of any job. Special consideration is given to maintaining a clean job site for both residential and professional interiors.

- *"He sticks to a schedule."*
- *". . . two very pleasant people to have work in your home. They are excellent with matching paint colors to wallpaper."*
- *"He hung and painted a ceiling medallion for a light fixture."*

George's Painting Company, (908)233-9798, A, 20 years in business

George does interior and exterior residential and commercial painting. He will custom-blend colors and "European Style" painting.

- *"George has done work in my house and it's not only beautiful but extremely creative. He is absolutely meticulous. Very recommendable."*
- *"All his workers are great. He has done many projects in our home. He painted our family room. We have always been happy with his work."*

Giordano Painting & Decorating Inc., (908)706-1066, A, 15 years in business

John Giordano is very versatile. His specialties include painting and wallpaper installation, applied arts such as custom murals, faux finishes and trompe l'oeil. No job is too old or new, large or small for this firm.

- *"He was just wonderful! Very punctual and neat . . . conscientious and very pleasant."*
- *"He did a lot of wallpapering and painting in our home. We were really pleased."*

James R. Higbie Fine Custom Painting, (908)580-1278, A, 15 years in business

This painter brings an eye for color to his business. His love of art (he has earned a BFA and MA in art education) enables him to look at a job from an artistic point of view. Both interior and exterior work is done and often he will be called upon to do unusual wall treatments such as glazing.

- *"He painted the inside and outside of our home. He's very dependable and did a great job. He does quality work."*

Hone Painting & Restoration Inc., (908)654-3878, UC MC SC MIC, 20 years in business

John Hone is well-known for restoration services including: paint stripping, plaster repair, fine wood restoration, wall and ceiling liners, Sheetrocking, papering, and interior and exterior painting. They work closely with the customer to satisfy quality and budget goals and offer a range of solutions to their painting problems and decorating needs.

- *"The paint was peeling off my old colonial house. Hone stripped the paint down to the wood, and after carefully repairing and preparing they gave us a beautiful paint job which has lasted for many years."*
- *"They are real master craftsmen."*

Interior Perfection, (908)654-1097, UC MC SC MIC, 3 years in business

As a one-man operation, Guy Mone oversees all aspects of his clients' needs from estimates to completion of interior painting and/or paperhanging. He prides himself on reliability, attention to detail and customer satisfaction therefore making the redecorating process less stressful and intimidating.

• *"He's great at wallpapering and patching wallpaper in problem areas."*
• *"He's a wonderful guy that knows how to prepare walls in old homes."*

J.C. Painting Service, (908)575-7484, UC MC SC MIC, 11 years in business

J.C. Painting prides itself on distinct attention to detail and providing customers with a dependable service. In addition to interior and exterior painting they also do sheetrocking, spackling and wallcoverings.
• *". . . very neat, conscientious."*
• *"Their attention to detail is commendable. He painted the entire inside and outside of our home. He also painted my mother's home."*

Landis Painting, (201)337-5559, MC SC WC, 2 years in business

Steve Landis made the switch! He went from being a corporate accountant to a painting contractor. He provides both interior and exterior painting and staining, full-power washing, faux finishes and and is a deck specialist.
• *"He's immaculate, reliable and honest."*
• *"I made him coffee everyday—he even sent me a thank-you note."*
• *"I enjoyed his choice of classical music while working!"*

M&W Painting, (908)654-3916, UC, 22 years in business

The two partners that own M & W Painting do interiors only. They provide services such as painting, wallcoverings, faux finishes and sponging.
• *"He's meticulous. He does beautiful preparation."*
• *"He matched existing paint from kitchen cabinets perfectly to do woodwork and trim in adjoining rooms."*

Mastercraft Painting & Wallcovering, (973)377-7448, UC MC SC WC, 40 years in business

Mastercraft is experienced in all types of coatings applicable to the residential and commercial paint market. Wallcovering installation ranges from commercial vinyls to beautiful residential papers. Company policy emphasizes that a clean, organized working environment be maintained on all job sites and in addition a nonsmoking policy is required for all interior work service.
• *"They were wonderful, creative and very helpful. They did all my wallpapering and some interior painting. The dining-room molding was repaired. He will do extras and takes special care of my possessions."*

PAINTERS

Park Painting & Wallpapering, (732)985-5732, A, 16 years in business

Park Painting is detail-oriented with their interior/exterior and wallpapering business. They are very proud of the fact that most of their business is obtained by "word-of-mouth."

- *"They are so trustworthy that we left our housekey and went to Maine for three weeks."*
- *" Even unsupervised they do a good job."*

Pine Manor Associates Inc., (973)377-6367, A, 40 years in business

The owner of Pine Manor Associates states that he was taught his skills by his father, who brought the trade from Italy. Preparation for a job includes plastering and repair. Areas of expertise are faux finishes, fabric and vinyl wallcovering installation.

- *"They not only did interior painting but they refinished my banister and did a beautiful job. They're very creative. I consider him an 'Old-World' master painter."*

Prime Painting, (973)676-8432, UC, 14 years in business

Dave Magliacane is a graduate of the U.S. School of Professional Paper Hangers in Rutland Vermont. He specializes in residential interior painting and paperhanging. Working along with decorators and carpenters, he can handle all facets of decorating from major wall repair to installation of handtrimmed wallpaper.

- *"Dave is very clean. His jobs are neat and completed to the 'nth' degree."*
- *"He takes pride in his work and it shows."*
- *". . . does extra work. If he sees it needs to be done he just does it."*

C. Scherer & Son, (908)688-7853, UC MC SC WC, 38 years in business

Frank Scherer defines himself as a painting and decorating contractor. In addition to interior and exterior painting, he also does paperhanging and restoration work.

- *"Frank has painted our house twice. He does a very thorough job and meets my most stringent criteria of neatness."*

St. Vincent Painting Co, (908)527-9000, UC MC, 12 years in business

Vincent Lavecchia is a residential contractor who will do both interior and exterior painting. His service is not advertised so his customer base is strictly from referrals. As quoted by Mr. Lavecchia: "If we don't do a great job for our clients we're sunk! So far we've been cruising!"

- *"He painted the outside of my house with no problems. He's fair about doing extra work."*

- *"He stripped off all the paint from an old porch and trim from the house around the windows. He did a great job of preparation."*

✍ _____

_____

Peter Steiner Painting & Decorating, (908)968-6529, UC SC MIC, 55 years in business

This is a third-generation "hands-on" type business providing complete interior and exterior service. All preparation and finished work are now being done by second-generation father and third-generation son. They provide a complete painting service both inside and outside.

- *"They painted both the inside and outside of my house. We were very satisfied."*
- *"He comes when he says he's coming and is very neat."*

✍ _____

_____

_____

Stephen's Painting and Wallpapering, (973)927-9245, MC SC WC, 7 years in business

A second-generation painter, Stephen cuts no corners when he does wallpapering, wallpaper removal, interior and exterior painting, wall repair and light Sheetrocking and spackling.

- *"He is meticulous. He knows all the pitfalls and issues of an old home and does a beautiful job with preparing old walls for wallpaper."*
- *"We have used him on our historic house and were amazed with the beautiful job he did with crumbling walls."*

✍ _____

_____

_____

Wallpaper Hang-ups, (908)218-9523, A, 27 years in business

This small company thrives on word-of-mouth from satisfied customers who they say seem to become more like friends. They do both interior and exterior painting and decorating for a range of homes, from those found in *Architectural Digest* to those found on "Any Street, U.S.A." Areas of expertise include wallcovering restoration and oil-based finishes.

- *"I had a difficult wallpaper and painting job. He put striped paper in a hall and up and down the stairs. It looks beautiful! He did an excellent job."*
- *"My house is old and crooked but the wallpaper job he did looks perfect."*

✍ _____

_____

_____

Welsh Painting & Decorating, (908)362-5978, MC WC, 17 years in business

This full-service business provides quality indoor and outdoor painting, staining, wallpapering, power washing and sandblasting. They strive to provide a courteous and high quality service.

- *"Matt is a wonderful guy and a great worker. He and his crew have painted my house twice in the last 10 years and my husband and I have always been pleased with the quality of his work."*

Mark Wills Painting, (908)272-1609, A, 17 years in business
Mark Wills Painting provides more than just interior/exterior painting of residential and commercial property. They do power washing and refinishing aluminum siding in addition to other services provided by painting contractors. All work is done by the company—there is no subcontracting so they feel they can provide a professional, high-quality job for the customer.

- *"My house had not been painted for eight years. It was very dirty on the outside. Mark and his crew spent time preparing, power washing, cleaning (gutters), spackling and scraping. The result is that now the house looks beautiful and because the job was done right we hope to go another eight years till our next job."*
- *"I would recommend him to my mother-in-law and that's saying something for him. He does excellent work and she's very picky."*

Steve Woomer Painting, (717)673-5643, A, 7 years in business
Steve Woomer concentrates on solving the customer's painting problems. He does custom residential work and will do both painting and wallpapering.

- *"He painted my hallway and also did exterior work. He's excellent and very honest."*
- *"He does good work. The best thing is I can leave him alone in my home and I trust him."*

John Wozniak Painting, (908)925-5453, A, 26 years in business
John specializes in sanding down and painting homes and commercial sites. He will also paint intricate trim work (gingerbread) in multiple colors. Special care is taken to provide a caring service for the customer's home or business.

- *"He's great! He painted my home and did a super job!"*
- *"He painted my store. I recommended him to at least a dozen people and they were all pleased with his work."*

PAINTERS

PEST CONTROL

Allison Pest Control, (732)938-4585, MIC, 80 years in business

This company provides termite and other pest control to homeowners in Southern Middlesex county and they will go into Ocean and Monmouth counties.

- *"I have been in the real estate business for very many years. It was back when I started using Allison for flea infestation in homes. They always did a wonderful job ridding these homes of fleas."*
- *"They are prompt, reliable and I will continue to use them."*

Alpha Pest Control Inc., (800)894-6569, UC SC MIC, 20 years in business

Alpha Pest Control is an independently owned company with service technicians having over 50 years of combined experience in the pest-control field. They offer safe, prompt and dependable service to homeowners and businesses and tailor these services to meet the customer's needs.

- *"I have used them for 15 years. They service me four times a year just to keep my house pest-free. They are prompt, neat and I can always rely on them. In addition they always remind me when an appointment is due."*

Atlas Termite and Pest Control, (908)233-7599, A, 10 years in business

A personalized program of residential pest control is provided by this small company. They are very thorough in treating the entire home to prevent or eliminate pests.

- *"I think he is fabulous! My daughter was having an immediate problem—in Morristown and he was up there in no time."*
- *"He is great for general exterminating and has done termite and carpenter-ant treatments. We have had no problems since."*

Buckingham Pest Control, (973)762-6760, UC, 30 years in business

With a personal touch, Buckingham will take care of many numerous problems such as ants, bees, cockroaches, crickets, fleas, rodents, termites and ticks.

- *"We've used them for four years and they are good! They do monthly maintenance outside and leave their bill in the mailbox. It's that easy!"*

Cooper Pest Control Inc., (609)799-1300, UC SC MC MIC, 42 years in business

Cooper Pest Control does not consider itself a traditional pest control company. Rather, they design programs that reduce pesticide exposure while solving pest problems. The primary method of solving pest problems is through knowledge of insect biology and behavior. Their main speciality is Integrated Pest Management which employs the use of nonchemical solutions. When pesticides are required IPM programs minimize the amount, toxicity and exposure. The Pest Proofing Division corrects physical conditions in the house which facilitate or are conducive to pest problems.

- *"We have been customers for eight or nine years. My husband also uses them for his place of work. They are reliable and neat. They will come within a reasonable amount of time."*
- *"If for some reason the problem isn't totally solved, they will return without hesitation."*

Crystal Pest Control, (908)722-1133, UC MC SC MIC, 25 years in business

Being a general household pest-control service, Crystal offers a friendly professional personalized service.

- *"They were recommended to me by my neighbor. They provide a quick service."*
- *"We live in a wooded area and consequently we have lots of little 'pesty' bugs. These people are trustworthy and pleasant and know how to deal with these unwanted creatures."*

Delsea Termite and Pest Control, (800)339-8515, A, 74 years in business

Delsea considers themselves experts in eliminating carpenter ants and termites. As an integrated pest-management company, customer safety and satisfaction are their number-one concern. All of their technicians are licensed by the NJ DEP and are continually educated in new techniques.

- *"My family has used this company for 12-and-a-half years in two homes we have owned. They will do monthly treatments for pests. They are reliable and will come in an emergency. I find them very flexible with scheduling."*

J. C. Ehrlich Co. Inc., (800)894-9130, A, 69 years in business

The J. C. Ehrlich Company has been protecting people and their environment since their founding in 1928. With 36 offices, in six states , they are the largest family-owned pest control company in the nation. They do not utilize "cookie cutter" approaches to pest control but rather use an Integrated Pest Management technique. State-certified personnel rely on extensive training to analyze each customer's situation.

- *"This company is professional and easy to work with. He came when we needed him. We had a problem with bees and since he worked on our home there have been no more bugs. They haven't come back and I consider that money well-spent."*
- *"We thought we had a problem with carpenter ants. Upon their inspection they found evidence of a problem. Their honesty was really appreciated for they didn't take advantage of us."*

Mantis Pest Control Inc., (800)870-5852, UC SC MIC, 27 years in business

As a small company that stands behind all their work, Mantis offers various services which include tree spraying for gypsy moths, inch worms and tent caterpillars. If you want to protect your deck from water damage, rot and decay from termites they offer a complete maintenance program. What about unwanted critters—mice, rats, squirrels, raccoons, skunks, opposums and bats? Let this company solve these problems.

- *"We use them for routine pest control. He sprays for ticks and fleas since I have animals."*
- *"He knows how much I do not like pesticides so he is exceptionally careful and does perimeters so my children don't have contact with the chemicals."*

Shuman's Termite and Pest Company, (973)376-2423, UC MC SC MIC, 7 years in business

Shuman's specializes in termite-control applications and inspections. Greg Shuman has personally treated over 5,000 homes for termites and wood-destroying insects.

- *"We have used Shuman's for years. Six times per year he is at my home on schedule to treat for mice. We live near a wooded area and the 'mouse situation' always exists, but at least he keeps it down to a minimum for us."*
- *"Whenever I need him he is there and many times he gets frantic calls from me for racoons, squirrels, flying squirrels, carpenter ants and a major problem with skunks. He is my hero! Plus he's a really nice guy. Anyone who uses Greg will not be disappointed."*

Simmons & Son Termite & Pest Control Inc., (908)757-3295, A, 27 years in business

This family-owned business provides reliable pest-control service to rid homes of termites, carpenter ants, wasps and bees.

- *"Simmons is dependable."*
- *"He does general exterminating in my home and we also own a rental apartment of which he does the same and rids these areas also of mice."*

Tarney Exterminating Co., (973)672-1616, A, 68 years in business

This professional pest-control company prides itself on protecting the health and property of their customers. Their clients range from residential and commercial to hospitals and government buildings.

- *"My parents used Tarney. I use him at my home and also my place of business."*
- *"Tarney has been a name in our family for 44 years. As a little girl I can remember him at our home. He is nice and pleasant and gets rid of mice, roaches, bugs, bees—you name it!"*

Viking Termite & Pest Control Inc., (800)618-BUGS, A, 19 years in business

Offering innovative approaches to pest problems, Viking uses all Integrated Pest Management methods available, including new termite baiting. Pest elimination is not just for the homeowner but also for business, hospitals, restaurants, nursing homes and food-processing plants. Specializing in termite and carpenter-ant control they use little or no pesticides.

- *"We have been using them for 10 years. We started with them when the company was small and now have expanded, but their service has remained the same—excellent!"*
- *"They are always pleasant on the phone, very accommodating with appointments and knowledgeable."*
- *"They are courteous about taking shoes off when needed. I get a postcard in the mail when it is time for the next maintenance call."*

_____

_____

_____

Westfield Exterminating Service Inc., (908)654-6648, A, 32 years in business

Westfield is a company dedicated to being environmentally responsible in solving pest problems safely and efficiently. They are specialists in termite and carpenter-ant elimination.

- *"We had a service that we were very happy with and then they closed their business. We went through several companies and we found this particular one which we are extremely satisfied with."*
- *"They know their stuff. They showed me pests that I was not aware of."*
- *"They treated for ants and I haven't seen any in years . . . told me if I do he would be back in a second."*

_____

_____

_____

PEST CONTROL

PIANO TUNING & REPAIR

deVré Piano Tuning & Repair Service, (908)561-9198, A, 35 years in business

Robert deVré was formerly with Steinway & Sons in New York. He does piano tuning and repair.

- *"I have used him for over 20 years. He is very much of the old school. Very knowledgeable and devoted to his instrument."*
- *"He's extraordinarily skilled and one of the finest in the area."*

Thomas G. Kaplan Piano Services, (908)995-2971, A, 10 years in business

Tom Kaplan's goal is to service the whole instrument. All brands of pianos are serviced but he is an authorized piano service technician for Yamaha Corp. (keyboard division). He will tune and provide complete piano action services such as rebuilding, regulation and Hammer voicing and tone regulating. Humidity control is also offered.

- *"Nice person. He did a good job tuning our piano."*

George Lachenauer, (908)241-8020, UC, 20 years in business

George started out as a concert pianist. He tunes and does action repair. All work comes from satisfied customer referrals.

- *"He has tuned our piano for years. He's not only an excellent piano player but an excellent tuner."*
- *"He definitely has a 'fine-tuned' ear. He's friendly and reliable."*

S. Minkoff Piano Shop, (201)460-7041, UC, 20 years in business

At Minkoff Piano Shop they believe a piano's continued performance depends on regular maintenance. With 20 years of experience in tuning and rebuilding pianos and over 30 years of playing the piano, he is experienced and qualified to bring out the best in your instrument. He specializes in electric, acoustic and player pianos. Steve's training at Steinway & Sons included tuning, regulating, tone regulating, stringing damper installation, pin blocks, and soundboard making.

- *"He's wonderful. He has tuned our piano for years and can fix any piano."*
- *"He's very knowledgeable with Steinways. He will also help if you are thinking of buying a piano by offering his expert opinion. He is a top-notch technician."*

Patella Piano Workshop & Studio Inc., (908)754-5891, A, 19 years in business

Fred will tune your piano with supreme skill and very high standards. Piano building and restoration are areas of expertise. He does restoration work all over the United States and Canada. Tuning is limited to the New York metropolitan area with the exception of instruments that have either been built or restored by his workshop.

- *"What do you say about your piano tuner? He's on tune! He is a nice guy and an excellent tuner. We have used him for five to six years. He also teaches piano."*
- *"Fred is a conservatory-trained pianist. He knows what the piano is supposed to sound like and would not tolerate less than the best. He has tuned and repaired our piano for the past six years and we feel very lucky to have found him."*

Phillips Piano Service, (908)665-2332, A, 32 years in business

As a member and past president of the New Jersey chapter of the Piano Technicians Guild, Douglas Phillips has a lot of experience in his field. He will not only tune pianos, but rebuild, repair, refinish and regulate. He specializes in residential, institutional and concert work.

- *"He will call you to schedule twice a year. He's a 'whiz' and wonderful. We have been using him for years and years."*
- *"We have used him for three years. He's very pleasant, reliable and nice."*

Dewey T. Rex, (908)757-0551, UC SC MIC, 32 years in business

It is refreshing to know that in this time of electronic gadgets, that Old-World craftsmanship can still be performed by the piano tuner/technician. Dewey Rex assures accurate piano action regulation by measurement and touch. He claims the piano-tuning business is a cross between an art and a science.

- *"He has been tuning our piano for years. He's reliable and will always send a postcard reminder when it is your piano's time to be tuned. He's a thorough professional of the 'old school.'"*
- *"He's devoted to the instrument and conscientious. We have used him for 20 years."*

Riedinger Piano Service, (732)560-1438, UC MC SC WC, 18 years in business

This piano tuner specializes in developing each instrument's highest potential to enable students, teachers and concert artists to reach greater levels of achievement. He will tune and repair but also transforms pianos—thought too far gone or beyond repair—to instruments of beauty, charm and value. He says oftentimes these older, seemingly worthless pianos can be resurrected producing very fine if not superior instruments.

- *"As far as I'm concerned, he's the best! An excellent piano tuner. He rebuilt my Baldwin piano. We have used him for several years to tune our piano and believe he is a fine tuner."*
- *"We have an antique baby grand that we bought from my daughter's piano teacher. He refurbished it, refinished it and it is absolutely beautiful. Not only is he a great piano tuner but he is able to repair and replace parts."*

PLUMBERS

American Standard Plumbing & Heating, Inc. (908)233-8666, UC, 7 years in business

This company provides clean, professional, quality workmanship. They are interested in working with customers to control costs and will provide flat rates up front. Their trucks are fully stocked and emergency service is available.

- *"His greatest strength is, when he says he'll be there he is."*
- *"His estimates are right in the boundaries of what he said."*
- *"Good plumber and good businessman!"*
- *"Over the years our whole family has used him."*

Bornstein Sons, Inc., (973)575-5050, UC MC WC MIC, 47 years in business

Bornstein Sons is a third-generation family-business serving New Jersey since 1950. All personnel are veteran technicians—they do not use subcontractors. Office is staffed from 7:15 a.m. and there is an after-hours answering service.

- *"Shows up on time as scheduled."*
- *"Can analyze the problem quickly."*
- *"We've had a very positive experience because of his good work."*

Robert A. Brydon Plumbing & Heating, (908)273-4179, UC MC, 40 years in business

Brydon does the traditional plumbing plus heating and air conditioning. All mechanics have been with the firm for many years and are encouraged to periodically brush up on their skills.

- *"We really like Brydon. They respond immediately to our phone calls. They come on time and over the five years we have used them we never have had a problem."*

Bryan Carisone Plumbing & Heating , (908)968-3941, SC MIC, 5 years in business

Bryan Carisone specializes in bathroom remodeling. In addition, these licensed plumbers will install, repair and service boilers and clean sewers and drains. Twenty-four-hour emergency service is available.

- *"Always calls back within a reasonable amount of time."*
- *"Don't have to chase after him."*
- *"Very neat, confident and competent!"*

Gerard J. Dinicola Plumbing & Heating, (908)233-7264, UC, 12 years in business

This plumbing firm concentrates on residential alterations and repairs. Every attempt is made to offer exceptional customer service done with quality workmanship and competitive pricing. Nancy Dinicola provides a human touch by personally answering all phone calls.

- *"These plumbers are the nicest people. From the time you call on the phone to the person they send out, they are extremely pleasant to deal with."*

✍ _____

_____

F.J. Domenick Plumbing & Heating, (908)232-3566, UC, 10 years in business
Domenick is an owner-operated and family-run business. They supply prompt and efficient service for all plumbing needs including repair and all other phases of plumbing and heating.

- *"Friendly guy . . . quick, clean, gets job done right the first time."*
- *"Tells it like it is!"*

✍ _____

_____

John Faber Plumbing & Heating, (908)322-7051, A, 10 years in business
"Service with a smile" is descriptive of this ten-year-old business. Their schedule is adjusted to the customer's needs. They specialize in bathroom remodeling and hot-water and steam boiler installations. Attention to cleanliness is a plus.

- *"Nice person to work with and pleasant to have in your home."*
- *"Clean, neat and always reliable."*

✍ _____

_____

Martin Feeney's Plumbing & Heating Inc., (908)396-0490, UC MIC, 15 years in business
Martin Feeney's employees are experienced plumbers, specializing in installation of hot-water heaters, sewer and drain cleaning, emergency repairs and custom bathroom and kitchen remodeling. When contacted they assure the customer the job will be done right the first time.

- *"A truly reliable plumber. He has helped us out so often I have lost count."*
- *"He installed our last hot-water heater. Did a great job and we have had no problems since."*

✍ _____

_____

Koegel Plumbing & Heating, Inc., (800)924-9758 , A, 38 years in business
Fred Koegel, in addition to general plumbing, is also a plumbing inspector. Areas of expertise include stain removal for tile, stainless steel and fixtures. Green toilet stains are no problem!

- *"Very dependable. Good work."*
- *"Impressive, well-supplied trucks. Responds quickly."*
- *"Has a storefront which displays products he uses."*

✍ _____

_____

Lindex Construction Company, (908)756-1455, A, 26 years in business
This company provides the highest quality service at competitive prices. They treat the

- *"Calls back instantly!"*
- *"Does great work . . . always pleasant!"*

Stafford Plumbing & Heating, (908)241-7067, UC, 20 years in business

Stafford is a plumbing and heating firm that provides service and renovations. They will also do sewer and drain cleaning.

- *"We have used him for years and find him reliable and adorable. He comes immediately if there is a problem."*
- *"He is a very nice person to have in my home and does good work."*

E.J. Stashluk & Sons, Inc., (973)635-0440, UC MC, 50 years in business

A business that has 80% repeat customers in the area is a true rarity. They have been in business for five decades providing diagnostic and design expertise for all plumbing needs.

- *"Able to address our concerns."*
- *"Finished the job in the time-frame stated."*
- *"Responsive to our needs."*
- *"Thorough . . . good cleanup job."*

Town Plumbing & Heating (Fosbre's), (908)968-1220, UC MC SC MIC, 47 years in business

A father and three sons have run this family business since 1950. They have the ability to do bath renovations, tile and Sheetrocking. Residential and commercial customers are welcome.

- *"Let me count the ways! We have had a good experience with them. On an emergency basis—day after Christmas—installed a furnace. Also corrected a backed-up septic . . . did a phenomenal job! Gets work done quickly. Returns call in a timely fashion. Neat, clean. Very, very satisfied."*
- *"We have been extraordinarily pleased with everything they have done. We lost our hot water at 8 A.M. and they were at my house by 9 A.M. to fix the problem. They also installed a new water-main line and had to dig under our lawn and sidewalk. When they were finished, there was no damage done at all. They left the place immaculate."*

Bruce Trano Plumbing & Heating, (908)654-3685, UC, 20 years in business

Trano Plumbing & Heating has been in business for 20 years. This owner-operator provides general plumbing and heating service to all customers.

- *"Truly dependable."*
- *"No muss, no fuss . . . just gets the job done well."*

- *"Very neat . . . part of the family!"*

✍🏻 _____

Valentine Plumbing, (732)635-3902, UC MC SC MIC, 23 years in business
This firm prides itself on reliability and honesty. Specialities are repairs, replacements and new installations. Pricing is by the job, not by the hour.
- *"Comes immediately."*
- *"Do not have to wait for service."*
- *"Very good at detecting and diagnosing problems. All repair work done with no problems afterwards."*
- *"Neat and clean."*

✍🏻 _____

Bill Whitney Plumbing & Heating, (908)689-7829, UC SC MC WC, 10 years in business
The customer will always receive a handshake from this general plumber upon completion of a job. All employees are encouraged to maintain customer satisfaction.
- *"Having an old house, he can anticipate what might happen to avoid any potential problem. Reliable. Always there when you need them. Wonderful!"*

✍🏻 _____

Willmar Plumbing & Heating Corp., (908)889-6646, A, 35 years in business
Willmar Plumbing has been providing exemplary, reliable service for over three decades. Customers are both residential and commercial and job scope includes repairs, renovation and new construction.
- *"Family business . . . very accountable."*
- *"Follow-up work is very important to us and he does this on a regular basis."*
- *"Good response time."*

✍🏻 _____

William Zepp & Son, Inc., (908)356-0745, SC MIC, 91 years in business
This plumbing and heating business was established in the year 1906. There aren't too many general plumbing businesses that can boast 90 years! They provide excellent service for both residential and light commercial customers.
- *"At times it can be difficult to find people who can work with older homes . . . he knows older homes!'*
- *" Has solved many of our plumbing problems."*
- *"Responsible."*

✍🏻 _____

POOLS

Action Pool Service & Supply Inc., (732)855-0044, UC MIC, 7 years in business

Action Pool is a complete service company for swimming pools. They open and close pools, maintain, replace lines and filters and install motors. A winter program is also available to the homeowner. A special plus is their retail store for all pool needs.

- *"We have used them for more than six years and never had any problems with their service. They service our pools at home and our beach house and we find them to be reliable in both places."*
- *"They do a wonderful job, are prompt at delivering supplies when we need them."*
- *"They have neat workers and can repair any problems. They open and close pools according to a schedule. Other family members use their services and are as happy as we are."*

Advantage Pools Inc., (908)604-0044, UC MC SC MIC, 8 years in business

Advantage builds, services and repairs swimming pools. They pride themselves on thoroughness and paying attention to details. Every service imaginable is offered from simple repairs to service packages and renovations.

- *"They are very good . . . very professional. They know exactly what they are doing."*
- *"They come on a schedule so I do not have to call. I really appreciate this."*

Anthony/Sylvan Pools, (732)752-0880, A, 50 years in business

This nationwide company has been constructing in-ground custom concrete pools for many years. Over 1000 pools have been built in this area alone by this company.

- *"Sylvan built a pool for us over 10 years ago. It has provided us with hours of pleasure. Their advice on placement was excellent and we have had no problems whatsoever with our pool. I would recommend them highly."*

Carlton Pools Inc., (908)685-1424, A, 25 years in business

Carlton is a family-owned-and-operated business. In addition to constructing pools, they will also service existing pools. All work is done by employees and subcontractors are never used.

- *"They have superior quality and design. Our pool is eight years old and we have had very few problems. They provide an excellent service."*

Cindy Pools Inc., (908)322-3997, UC MC SC MIC, 40 years in business

Building and servicing pools is this company's mainstay. They have been well-known in the area for over four decades.

- *". . . built one pool about 30 years ago for us. They have maintained it for us ever since with no significant problems."*
- *"They are very reliable and they even come in cold weather to make repairs."*

Country Pool and Spa, (732)805-9011, UC MC SC MIC, 3 years in business

This young company provides all types of service on existing pools. They associate personally with the customer in order to determine individual needs regarding care and upgrade of their pool. All service is performed as if they were the customer and the pool was their own.

- *". . . very responsive. They come every week and maintain my pool."*
- *"They have a lot of experience and know exactly what to do without being told."*

Countryside Pools, (908)832-2005, MC SC, 8 years in business

If you want your pool crystal clear, Countryside Pools can help you achieve this. They will maintain and repair your pool if needed, add filtration, piping and leak detection. Customer service is a priority and they are very willing to give advice and work with clients to fulfill specific needs.

- *"I have used them for five years. They are efficient, dependable and totally great to have around."*
- *"They always strive to do the right thing to make us happy . . . and they like my dogs!"*

D & B Pools Inc., (908)725-8819, SC, 15 years in business

A family-owned company, D & B provides a complete service opening and closing pools, major and minor repairs and sales and installation. They will work on either in-ground or above-ground pools. Water testing and analysis is free.

- *"D & B has serviced our pool for eight years. They have saved me a lot of time and effort with chemicals and keep our pool looking beautiful."*
- *"He always gives us good advice which we appreciate and is very dependable with maintenance. We can recommend him highly."*

Jayson Pool Service, (908)688-1111, A, 60 years in business

Jayson is a full-service pool company providing customers with water purification, water conditioning and service. Their specialty includes installation of in-ground concrete pools.

- *". . . have provided our service annually as well as weekly for the past 12 years. They open and close at the beginning and end of each summer season. They are an absolute pleasure . . . prompt and friendly service is a constant. Without hesitation Jason is #1."*

L & S Pool and Spa Service, (973)538-8144, A, 27 years in business

L & S has been involved in the spa industry from its beginning starting with the California wooden hot-tubs. They work on a variety of pools such as Army bases, municipal pools, country clubs, colleges as well as residential pools. They have also built religious baths including Baptismal fonts and mitzvahs. Spa and sauna construction are also included in their services.

- *"Oh, he's the best! He really is! He can always fit me in his schedule I never have to wait."*
- *"He opens and closes our pool and has installed filters and a vacuum system."*
- *"We have used him for three years and my husband once said, 'Why didn't we find him 10 years ago?'"*

P.M. Swimming Pool Service, (908)322-3992, A, 18 years in business

P.M. is a full-service pool business with 24-hour service trucks. Their trucks are radio-controlled for fast emergency service. Available to the customer are openings and closings, expert leak detection, weekly service, major pool renovation, replacement in-ground liners and all repairs. As an authorized Anthony/Sylvan service center, they are also an authorized warranty station for almost all major pool equipment manufacturers.

- *"We have used them for the past nine years. They replastered an existing 19-year-old pool, redid the deck and installed new plumbing. All this was done completely to our satisfaction."*
- *"They installed and new heater and filter in our pool. We have always been pleased with their service as have my friends that use them."*

Richards Swimming Pool Service, (908)725-4444, MC SC MIC, 37 years in business

This authorized Anthony/Sylvan Service Dealer will provide pool service and parts and equipment.

- *". . . very responsive. They know what they are doing. They come on schedule every year and are very reliable about it. They are very careful about plantings around the pool."*

Sum'r Fun Pool Service, (973)379-9302, UC MC, 18 years in business

No matter how busy the day is at Sum'r Fun, no customer is ever rushed off the phone or out of the office. All pool services are done by this family-owned company and they say that they actually can't wait till spring to talk with their customers again.

- *"They are extremely reliable and easy to work with."*
- *"We have used them for years and I find that they have great respect for my property in addition to taking good care of my pool."*

✍ _____

_____

_____

Superior Pool Service Inc., (908)232-6963, A, 11 years in business

At Superior Pool, catering to customers is important. In addition to opening and closing, they will do vacuuming, skimming and brushing of the walls, emptying the skimmer basket and backwashing the filter (if needed) on a weekly basis. Proper chemicals are added to the water as needed. A winter cover maintenance is also available.

- *"They are, as we speak getting our pool ready for the summer. Their name is what it says . . . superior!"*
- *"We have been using them for eight years and they are reliable, honest and nice. They are always willing to put extra time in if needed."*

✍ _____

_____

_____

POOLS

REAL ESTATE INSPECTION

Eastern Integrated Services Corp., (908)232-1166, A, 10 years in business

Eastern realizes the importance of getting things done on a timely basis. Their goal is to provide the customer with the information needed to be be comfortable in their new home. Their inspectors are fully trained and possess all required state and local licenses necessary to conduct home inspections. An inspection by Eastern includes: roof and exterior, basement and structural, heating and cooling, plumbing, electrical, appliances, interior walls, floors and ceilings, fireplaces, windows and doors, attic, insulation, and grading.

- *"They provided the most comprehensive home inspection we have ever had. This is a great service. They can always give me an appointment when I need it."*
- *"As a realtor I have used them for several properties recently. I now know why they have been used by my office exclusively for several years. They are available evenings and all day. Saturday appointments really work with my busy schedule. I can always count on them."*

Empire Inspection Inc., (800)235-6090, A, 11 years in business

Empire is a firm of professionals who will assist real estate buyers who wish to have detailed facts regarding the condition of any property. They provide easily understood reports on electrical and mechanical systems as well as structural and roofing conditions. Reports on water seepage, termite and/or carpenter ant infestation, plumbing systems, chimneys and flues, insulation, fire hazards and more are provided to the client. They also offer radon, lead and asbestos testing. They will provide oral and written reports of their findings.

- *"We have used them three times. Very reliable and gave us extremely detailed reports."*

Foresight Engineering, (973)377-0600, A, 13 years in business

The professional engineers from Foresight have had extensive experience in home inspection. They will investigate structural engineering and do radon testing and mitigation.

- *"Very thorough. They are interested in detail. When we were purchasing our home he realized there was something wrong with the septic system. To our benefit, the system had to be 'replaced.' We are so glad he caught it. He paid attention to our interests."*

H & J Freile Home Inspections, (800)581-1887, A, 10 years in business

Information about the property being purchased will not only help the customer enjoy a more comfortable and safer home but will also help to protect a major financial investment. In addition to structural inspections, Freile offers an extended line of inspections and tests that help the home buyer to intelligently determine the condition of the property. These inspections include: electrical, plumbing, heating and cooling, termite infestation, radon testing, water testing and more. Their reporting system provides the client with an easy-to-read report which details all major systems and structures plus a summary of all major repairs.

- *"Excellent. They were recommended to us years and years ago by our realtor. We have used them on two moves. They are very thorough and the end product is a huge binder with all the information but it also includes what to look for in any home you are buying."*

Inspect A Home Inc., (973)379-4124, A, 22 years in business

The complete home inspection is performed by this company. This will include the evaluation of the structure, interior systems and several additional services. Every inspector is a member of the American Society of Home Inspectors and they must fulfill annual education requirements.

- *"He was a nice guy and he did a good job."*
- *"A thorough job. He covered everything that needed to be. My husband and I both liked the way he conducted himself."*

Westfield Home Inspection Service Inc., (908)233-6029, A, 16 years in business

Ralph Defiore provides this service to help people form a judgment on purchasing a home. His inspection will point out all structural problems that may exist. He will make recommendations on maintenance and give life expectancies on existing systems. A detailed report is available in 48 hours.

- *"He's terrific, very reliable. He's conscientious and knows what he's doing. Being in the real estate business, I have known and used Ralph for 20 years. Some of my clients have used him two to three times and keep coming back."*

REAL ESTATE INSPECTION

A & M Roofing Co., Inc., (908)638-8326, UC MC SC WC, 15 years in business

A & M Roofing does not advertise its services. All business is obtained from previous satisfied customers. They work on all types of roofs, including slate, cedar, shingle and cedar ply rubber roof systems which are used primarily for flat roofs. Often when working on a roof, other minor problems such as caulking and missing shingles will be corrected free-of-charge. This is their way of developing customer loyalty.

- *"We have used him for three homes we have built. Not only is he good at his work but he is trustworthy and dependable. He will come back if there is a problem even if it is eight years later."*

BBJ Inc., (908)356-7441, A, 15 years in business

BBJ is a full-service firm with expertise in all areas of roofing. The customer is provided with distinctive guidance from a very experienced staff.

- *"They did a fabulous job. They took the roof all the way down to the beams. The roof did not have plywood, so they had to put in plywood to bring it up to code. They are excellent!"*

W. Caswell Home Improvements, (908)722-9548, A, 30 years in business

When using this small family business, the homeowner always deals with the owner who does all the work—using no subcontractors. He does one job at a time until completion. Final payment is not due until the job is finished and the customer is completely satisfied.

- *"Bill did some flat roof work on our house. We were very pleased that it lasted longer than he said it would for flat roofs do need work more frequently."*
- *"We are quite pleased with him. He is a nice guy and does good work."*

R. T. Corbet Roofing & Siding, (732)528-8994, UC MIC, 11 years in business

The main goal of R. T. Corbet is keeping the customer's house watertight by providing quality roofing, siding and windows. To make roofing watertight they use underlayments before the first shingle or siding is installed. Being competitive their main goal is quality and service. They pride themselves on their response time to problems.

- *"They are reliable and responsible. They were able to do my roofing job within a reasonable amount of time with no problems."*

Komar Roofing Inc., (908)232-6383, UC, 22 years in business

The owner of this one truck–one crew business works on each and every job with his three employees. They will tackle any roof and place a tremendous emphasis on quality work.

- *"We had a section of our roof that was not pitched correctly—it is basically flat. He put on a rubberized all-weather roof to prevent leakage . . . especially when we have a heavy snowfall. We've had no problems since."*
- *"They are very neat and prompt. They come immediately when we have had problems and they stand by their work."*
- *"We have used him for 12 years. He put two completely new roofs on two of our homes. We have had no problem since. He is reliable, trustworthy and does excellent work."*
- *"We own a home in Florida which needed a new roof. I gave the estimate to Mr. Komar to ask him if this was a fair price, because we do not live there all year. He reviewed it for us and gave us a lengthy opinion. We feel this was above and beyond the call of duty and we would recommend him very highly."*

Russ Naylor Roofing, (908)668-8169, UC SC MIC , 9 years in business

This roofer works alone. He specializes in slate and leak repairs, residential tear-offs and reroofing.

- *". . . very accurate. Really good one-man operation."*
- *"He is meticulous. He's a slate-roof specialist and there aren't many of them out there."*
- *"We had a bad leak problem. He took each slate off, one by one, and stacked accordingly so they would go back in the same spot. He did not try to mask the problem but took each slate off until he found the source of the leak."*

John Novalis Roofing Co., (973)377-1523, MC, 34 years in business

A "one-man show," Novalis does residential roofing of all types. They hand-nail all new roofing and also provide a gutter service with their own gutter machine.

- *"The best roofer around! He replaced one entire shingled roof and hammered each nail in himself in every individual shingle. That is why we chose him."*

Pangborn Roofing Inc., (732)572-0534, A, 21 years in business

Collectively, these two brothers and their father have 100 years of experience. Their services include roofing, reroofing, repairs, slatework, gutters, leaders flat roofs, shingles and leak repair. Ninety percent of their work is obtained from satisfied customers.

- *"They are one of the few roofers who will work on slate roofs. They have done a lot of detail work on our roof. There were slates missing that needed to be replaced and he searched and was able to match our slate beautifully."*
- *"They are very detail-oriented and extremely reliable. They do an exceptionally fine job."*

Ernest Perrella Contractors, (973)292-6808, UC MC, 28 years in business

Flat roofs and chimney repairs are the specialities of this small firm.

- *"I have used him for many years. Whenever there is a problem, he's there!"*
- *"He comes quickly and is very thorough."*

✍ _____

_____

_____

Scotchwood Construction, (732)316-2440, UC MIC, 10 years in business

This owner-operator works on every job himself. Subcontractors are never used. He does roofing, vinyl siding and vinyl replacement windows.

- *"He is very polite. He comes when scheduled. I appreciate his honesty. One section of the roof really didn't need any work and he told us that."*

✍ _____

_____

_____

SECURITY SYSTEMS

ADT Security Services, inc., (201)804-2280, A, 120 years in business
For over a century ADT has been in the business of making homes and businesses safe. They install all types of security systems and have a vast service and repair business.
- *"Highly professional."*
- *"Very competent."*

American Detection Systems, Inc., (908)687-2929, A, 10 years in business
A distinct reason why this company feels that people should do business with them is that they are small enough to understand the customers' needs—but large enough to service all their requirements. They are commercial and residential security and fire alarm specialists.
- *"Very reliable."*
- *"Prompt service whenever we have any kind of problem."*

C & N Security Systems, (973)875-7808, A, 15 years in business
No job is too small or too big for C & N Security. Installation of security systems, fire alarms, intercoms, closed-circuit televisions, cable and phone jacks are part of the many services offered. Satisfied customers make them very happy.
- *"Have used him for three years and we think they are a very good company. They do neat work."*
- *"They installed our system and maintain it. They are absolutely very honest and trustworthy."*

Diversified Home Installations, Inc., (908)850-5400, A, 10 years in business
Diversified specializes in the supply and installation of security systems and intercoms among many other things. Many decisions need to be made in wiring the home and installing these built-in systems. They take the time to determine the customer's needs so that the final system conforms to lifestyle requirements.
- *"They were recommended to me by our builder. They did a good job with installation of an alarm system which is hooked up to a central station that is completely monitored."*
- *"They do much more than alarm systems. They wired our entire home for alarm, stereo, surround-sound and television. They do state-of-the-art stuff. They did a fabulous job and we recommend them very highly."*

Haig's Service Corporation, (908)968-6677, A, 25 years in business
With many years of experience in the installation of burglar and fire alarm systems, this

company has the ability to satisfy any customer's needs. This is a second-generation family-operated business.

- *"Professional. Detail-oriented and they know how to work in old homes."*
- *"We have used them for six years and would highly recommend them."*

Holmes Protection, (212)760-0630, A, 138 years in business

Founded in 1858, Holmes has continued to lead the electronic security industry by using innovative and creative products. Holmes secures both residential and commercial facilities through access control, fire, and burglar detection, closed-circuit television, vehicle tracking, wireless transmission systems and interactive alarm verification. They provide a full range of services including installation, service, inspection and monitoring.

- *"They service our system once a year. They are dependable and extremely honest and trustworthy."*
- *"We have been using them for over 10 years and I especially like the central station people who call if the alarm has gone off (accidentally or otherwise). They are extremely polite and make you feel like they are truly concerned about the customer's safety."*

Homeguard Alarms & Monitoring Inc., (908)946-7882, UC MC SC MIC, 16 years in business

In these times, a selection of home or business security system is a very important decision, and Homeguard has been offering burglar and fire alarm installations and monitoring services to hundreds of satisfied customersfor over 15 years. Their product line is state-of-the-art and certified personnel strive to provide customers with prompt efficient, quality workmanship.

- *"I would describe them as dependable monitoring. We have been using them for eight years with great satisfaction. Excellent service."*

Pride Alarms, Inc., (201)343-9201, A, 20 years in business

How important it is to be knowledgeable about your industry and understand the laws and zoning in the communities you service. Pride Alarms have the ability to use that knowledge when installing burglar and fire alarm systems, cameras, phone systems and intercoms for both residential and commercial customers.

- *"Very reliable. They always return my phone calls."*
- *"They are consistent with accommodating me very nicely to schedule when it is convenient for me. They do nice work and are very helpful."*

Pro Tech Check Systems, (908)561-6666, UC SC MIC, 20 years in business

Pro Tech, established in 1976, installs and services systems for loss prevention and life protection. They install personal panic systems, emergency response systems, intercoms and observation systems (CCTV). Also provided are direct police and fire department connections and 24-hour alarm monitoring via a central station.

- *"This is an owner-operated firm. He is very quick to come out when you need him. I find it very comforting when I am dealing with one person for security reasons."*
- *"Very reliable. I can call him any time—morning, afternoon or night. He is readily available."*

Stahl Security Systems, (800)560-5262, A, 15 years in business

This firm will repair and monitor older alarm systems as well as newer high-tech systems. They provide a personalized service that is geared to satisfy each customer.

- *"They installed our security system. We have had no problems. He returned to rewire certain closets when my rabbit ate through the wires. They provide a good service."*
- *"They are very pleasant and reliable. They were recommended to me by a friend and I would recommend them highly."*

Superior Security Systems, (732)563-0605, A, 8 years in business

The customer will never get a "hard sell" from Superior because they do not use salespeople. All types of security systems are provided including burglar and fire alarms. Twenty-four hour central station monitoring is offered.

- *"Very professional and sensitive to the job. They are neat and cleaned up everything. They snaked wires through walls and hid wires very effectively. He was able to go through plaster without cracking the walls."*
- *"They respected the integrity and architecture of our home."*

Systemtech Inc., (908)925-4363, A, 28 years in business

Systemtech does custom installation of both residential and commercial security systems and telephone systems. It might be fun to ask them in which celebrity homes they have installed alarms.

- *"With this type of business you want someone in your home who is honest. He is very honest! He does a great job. We give him a ton of business."*
- *"He installed alarm systems in two of our homes and also smoke and carbon monoxide detectors . He installed telephone lines and did a wonderful wiring job that was well-hidden."*
- *"He was recommended to me very highly and has done our neighbor's system and also my husband's place of business. He is great returning phone calls."*

Ultimate Security Systems Inc., (973)535-0515, A, 18 years in business

A personal dimension of service to each and every client. They never lose sight of the most important part of every protection, the life safety of the people involved. Each system, burglary alarm, closed-circuit television and card-access systems, and executive protection program is unique to itself, not cut from a mold and merely set in place as you find all too often in today's impersonal world.

- *"Wonderful, reliable. I am impressed with their state-of-the-art equipment."*
- *"Our family has been using this company for 20 years, with much success."*

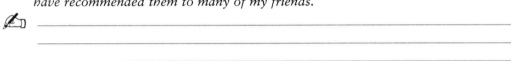

Whitehouse Security Services, (908)534-9093, MC SC, 11 years in business

Whitehouse offers all types of electronic security systems for residential properties.

- *"Excellent. They wired for our burglar and stereo system and both jobs were rather complicated. They are likeable, friendly and have a good response time. I have recommended them to many of my friends."*

Aqua Magic Lawn Sprinklers Inc., (908)974-2442, U, 20 years in business

This family-owned business strives to provide quick response time for service and repair. Their employees have years of experience in irrigation systems. Not only do they install new systems but will repair damaged and worn systems.

- *"We have used them for 10 years. They are prompt and courteous."*
- *"They maintain both our sprinkler in our house and our beach home—they're nice to deal with in both places."*

Eco Systems, Inc., (732)679-7474, UC SC MIC, 16 years in business

Eco Systems wants to be involved in creating a beautiful environment for the homeowner. They will install custom lawn sprinkler, sump pump and drainage systems. An added specialty is the design and installation of "Nightscape" lighting system.

- *". . . installed our sprinkler system eight years ago. We had sodded our lawn prior to the job and they were exceptionally careful and did no damage to the lawn."*
- *"They are very reliable. Our system was installed on time. I would highly recommend them."*

Emerald Lawn Sprinklers, (973)376-7753, A, 20 years in business

As their name implies, Emerald installs underground sprinkler systems that keep the lawn as green as their name.

- *"I am so thrilled that we now have an underground sprinkler system. We used to water on our own which was so time-consuming. Now, I do not have to worry about sprinkling at all and my grass always looks beautiful."*

Green Park Company Inc., (908)241-8198, A, 30 years in business

Green Park installs all major manufacturers' equipment. They will suggest the equipment most applicable to your site, keeping in mind which systems have developed a fine service track record. Because service is so important this company is open seven days a week from March 1 to December 15.

- *"They did a complicated job of installation much to our satisfaction."*
- *". . . did a fine job. They respond promptly and are very efficient. Over the four years we have used them, they have provided us with good service."*

Hydro-Tek Ltd., (908)276-1062, A, 5 years in business

Hydro-Tek has two slogans: "We cater to you" and "Are you wet yet?" If you answered no to the second question you need Hydro-Tek! They are irrigation and lawn sprinkler

SPRINKLER SYSTEMS

experts and will make sure their systems meet all customer requirements.

- *"We use them for maintenance and turning our system on in the spring and off in the fall. They are reliable and helpful and can repair any problems to my satisfaction."*

Lawn Irrigation, (732)382-4554, A, 30 years in business

This family-owned company will service and install sprinkler systems. They strive to provide excellent service by using quality equipment.

- *". . . have used them for many years. We find them to be honest, dependable and reliable. They turn the system on beginning of spring and turn it off when the season ends. We have never really had any problems."*

Oasis Sprinkler, (908)968-9116, UC SC MIC, 12 years in business

Professional lawn sprinklers designed for the homeowner's landscape needs are installed and serviced by this company. Approximately 85% of all their new installations arise from established customers' recommendations.

- *". . . installed our sprinkler system three years ago. They are very knowledgeable and extremely dependable. They have great response time to my phone calls."*
- *"They are very friendly and were exceptionally careful when installing the system to take care of my property."*

Phoenix Irrigation Corp., (973)912-9800, A, 50 years in business

This irrigation system company puts service of existing customers' systems first. Installation is important but a quality service plan is their optimum goal and what they feel sets them apart from other companies.

- *"They come on time, are dependable and call ahead to schedule appointments. They're very flexible with my schedule."*
- *"I have used them for three years and am very satisfied. They are always on top of everything. They pay personal attention which is very important to me. I have recommended them to my son who has a new home and he is thrilled."*

Princeton Landscape Irrigation Specialists Inc., (609)581-9550, A, 20 years in business

Princeton Landscape Irrigation would like their clients to know that their commitment is to provide each and every one with results, regardless of the scope of the project. They install systems not only for the homeowner but for commercial and industrial sites as well.

- *"They are reliable. They've been in business for years and definitely care about property. They're very well-known in our area."*

R & R Irrigation, (908)968-2990, UC MC SC MIC, 26 years in business
R & R designs, installs, and services underground sprinkler systems.
- *"They provide great service. In the fall they shut the system down and drain. In the spring the system gets turned on and all zones are checked to see if they are running properly. They are very service-oriented."*
- *"When we moved in our house several years ago, it had not been taken care of and many things had to be repaired including the existing sprinkler system. They took a totally defunct system and had it working perfectly. A great service!"*

Service Pro, (908)233-0368, A, 16 years in business
By using a 24-hour beeper system this company can quickly respond to all problems. They provide a service that is respectful of the customer's existing property. Personal one-on-one appointments with the owner/operator are available.
- *"They are reliable. They explain everything in detail and respond quickly to service calls."*

The Sprinkler System Inc., (973)379-3220, UC MC SC MIC, 25 years in business
Because an underground sprinkler system is a "blind item sale" (the customer doesn't actually see it), this owner-operator tries to install well thought-out, efficient systems. Quality of work is important because installation is underground and this company wants the system to be easily serviceable.
- *"We have a well and two acres of land, which meant that we had a lot of area to cover and did not want to take too much water from the house while the sprinklers were in use. They installed many zones and we have them run at different times so it does not pull from the house."*
- *"Our neighbors used other sprinkler companies and were experiencing sprinklers just spitting out because they were not installed the way this company does it. Needless to say, they were unhappy."*

Treasure Lawns Inc., (800)570-7226, A, 25 years in business
Treasure Lawns designs and incorporates the most comtemporary installation techniques. Their sprinklers are designed to satisfy the watering requirements of your lawn, increase its beauty and insure that your lawn will last. A Treasure Lawn underground automatic sprinkler system makes the lawn-care easy, convenient and economical.
- *"Due to the sun, our grass was browning and we were losing our shrubs. This was all corrected by the installation of the sprinkler system. They were very careful with our property and did a beautiful job. They are very accommodating."*
- *"After they installed our sprinkler system our shrubs and lawn look wonderful. They also provide a wonderful service for opening and closing the system. I would very much like to recommend them."*

TILE

Decoratta Ornamental Terracotta, (215)453-0820, A, 12 years in business

Decoratta creates custom handmade tiles. They claim their tiles are like nothing found anywhere else. Unique in color and design, they can be fabricated to fit into a variety of environments such as mosaic floors, walls, fireplaces and garden accents.

- *"Their work is incredibly unique. I don't think anyone else can do slate and ceramic floors like they do."*
- *"They are organized and neat and do exactly what they say they will do. They are incredibly talented and reliable."*

Tom DiNizo Tile & Marble Contractor, (732)563-1889, UC SC, 20 years in business

This tiler will install ceramic tile and marble. He will consult and advise the customer, if needed, concerning placement and design.

- *"We found Tom through friends of ours. We left him alone one summer to redo the basement floor and bathroom in black and white. He was very creative with the installations of the tile in the bathroom. He angled the tile on the basement floor to make it look larger."*
- *"Anyone who uses Tom should be very happy. We were thrilled with his work."*

Michael G. Ellis, (908)322-9329, UC, 18 years in business

Mike will install ceramic tile and marble for floors, walls and countertops. He claims his work to be "a thing of beauty" and communication with the customer is very important.

- *"Mike is a great guy. He really knows what he's doing. He has tiled both our bathroom (master) and kitchen. The end result was more than we expected. It's truly a pleasure to spend time in these rooms now."*

Genna Tile Contractors, (973)661-5172, A, 38 years in business

Genna offers personal artistic service. They are a third-generation business and will do residential and commercial ceramic tile and marble installation. They believe a happy customer lasts forever.

- *"He was fantastic. Did a great job. Extremely cooperative. I had very unusual decorative tiles—he would put them up but did not immediately grout so that when I came home at night if there were any changes to be made, he would do it the next day. He would phone me at night to make sure I was happy."*
- *"An excellent tile man. Because I was at work while he was working in my home, I would leave him notes and he would always respond."*

184

Grand Marble & Tile, (908)479-4188, A, 23 years in business

This company will install ceramic tile, marble and granite. They also do fabrication of all pieces and accessories. After installing they will do necessary maintenance and restoration or repair if damage occurs.
- *"Very professional. Excellent work. Very personable."*
- *"He is dependable. He did an enormous amount of tilework in our home and he does a superb quality job."*

Magliacano Tile & Marble Co., (908)964-7032, A, 24 years in business

Matt Magliacano listens to his customers and customizes each job to their lifestyle and design requirements. He will install ceramic tiles, marble and granite for floors, walls, ceilings, bathrooms, kitchens and patios using only the best of materials.
- *"Matt installed a granite countertop in our kitchen. I love it for it not only looks great but is low maintenance. His tilework is to perfection for his grouting is very carefully done."*

Norman Martina Tile, (973)543-6263, MC SC, 32 years in business

A training in art and working as an art teacher prepared Norman Martina for the aesthetic aspect of tile and marble installation. He apprenticed with his father and uncle and feels he brings a high level of expertise to each job. He is an expert with the renewed wave of profile borders, intricate layouts and patterns.
- *"He installed all the tile in our new home. This included bathrooms, kitchen kitchen floor, mudroom etc. He's very artistic and comes up with his own designs."*
- *"When we built our new home the tile installer really did not do a good job. Norm was recommended to me by all my neighbors and he came and fixed this other guy's mistakes. I haven't had a problem since. We're sorry we didn't use him in the first place."*

Flavio Trani & Son, (732)381-7324, A, 48 years in business

This ceramic-tile and marble contractor does residential work tailored to the customer's wants and needs. Helping the homeowner design and renovate they strive for excellence. They do kitchens, bathrooms, foyers and repairs.
- *"They are just the best workers. I have known and used them for 25 years.*
- *They go above and beyond."*
- *"Real craftsmen. Once they lay the tile there are never any problems. They look ahead and know exactly what to do."*

UPHOLSTERERS

Aravena's Upholstery, (908)298-0480, A, 29 years in business

Aravena's will guarantee all their fabrics and work. This business will do upholstery and antique-furniture restoration. From problems like torn or faded vinyl or leather upholstery to antique furniture that needs to be stripped and refinished, they can fulfill the customers' requirements. Upholstery cleaning is available on request.

- *"He reupholstered chairs and sofas for our family room. We were so pleased—he did a quality job."*
- *"He has done a lot of reupholstering for us and my impression is that he always wants to please his customers. I use him over and over."*

Edwards Furniture Restoration, (973)635-2468, MC 22 years in business

Gary Edwards inherited his father's perfectionism and he feels it shows in his workmanship. His family has been in the upholstery business for three generations and their speciality is reupholstering antique furniture.

- *"Such a gem. A really true craftsman—he learned the business from his father."*
- *"I am so glad he wants to be in this book. He has upholstered many pieces for me and I found him pleasant to work with. He does beautiful quality work."*

Fernando Upholstery, (973)467-3767, A, 33 years in business

Fernando Upholstery specializes in antiques, leather and tufting—although they will tackle any kind of furniture. All work is meticulously hand-done.

- *"They did everything quickly and right on time as promised."*
- *"I find them pleasant to work with and no problems at all. Real quality work."*

Jan's Antiques, (908)654-4150, A, 12 years in business

Jan's does upholstery, restoration and refinishing of newer furniture and also antique repair and restoration. They will also aid the customer in appropriate fabric selection.

- *"Over the years I have purchased antique chairs from them and had them reupholstered. They do beautiful, meticulous work. They're a delight to deal with—careful with every detail. Quick phone response and they will pick up and deliver."*
- *"Several years ago a very close friend was sitting in my living room smoking a cigar. Somehow an ash fell and burned a hole in the armchair he was sitting in. Jan's reupholstered the chair beautifully; we like it better than the original and the best part is that our friend paid for it. We have now named the chair in his honor."*

Romeros Upholster and Design Center, (732)906-6622, A, 14 years in business

Romeros is dedicated to the highest standards of quality and customer satisfaction. Customers can choose fabrics from a huge selection offered in their showroom. They do custom reupholstery and restyling of all types of furniture including antiques. All work is performed on the premises. Free consultation is offered in the customer's home.

- *"They have reupholstered many of my pieces including several of my favorite antiques. They were easy to work with and I loved their fabrics."*
- *"They give wonderful advice and have a sixth sense about fabrics."*

Roselle Upholstery, (908)245-4756, UC, 14 years in business

At Roselle Upholstery "quality is job one." They reupholster old and new furniture.

- *"They have done all the upholstery work in my home. When I discovered him he was redoing a chair for the Newark Museum. He does beautiful museum-quality work."*
- *"He can literally do a chair within two to three weeks—which is a big plus!"*

Stirling Interiors, (908)647-1530, UC MC SC, 7 years in business

As a custom-upholstering business, Stirling can honestly say that they respond to their customers with excellent service and good quality. Both high-end and more reasonably priced fabrics are provided for the customer to select. Window treatments are also available.

- *"They covered an antique chair for me. It is absolutely beautiful, a job done to perfection. It was all done very quickly."*
- *"They are delightful to deal with—very helpful in choosing the right fabric."*

Ultimate Upholstery & Drapery, (973)378-5924, UC, 9 years in business

The quality of their workmanship and the ability to use coil springs when constructing on custom wood is the ultimate speciality of Ultimate.

- *"They are real nice people. They picked up and redelivered the furniture. They were very careful when moving my pieces."*
- *"They have many fabric samples to choose from. They even refinished the wood on my upholstered piece. I would definitely use them again."*

Zelaya Interiors, (201)868-3818, A, 15 years in business

Zelaya does upholstery and more. Every job is custom-made and attention is paid to all customer requests. They need two to three weeks lead time on all jobs.

- *"Professional, reliable and fast."*
- *"He can bring to life any design ranging from a sketch to a magazine cutting. I have had a wonderful experience working with them. Their follow-up service is excellent. I cannot say enough about them."*

UPHOLSTERERS

Cymes Painting, (908)289-8363, UC, 4 years in business

The home-improvement speciality of Cymes Painting includes interior painting wallpapering, Sheetrocking, plastering and spackling. When calling ask for Kazik!

- *"He's used a lot in my neighborhood—sort of the neighborhood painter!"*
- *"He did a great job, was clean and neat and we were completely satisfied."*

D & D Painters, (908)968-6549, UC SC MIC WC, 18 years in business

D&D does extensive interior wallpapering and decorative painting such as texturized finishes, staining and pickling. They also specialize in faux finishes, rag, sponges, marbleizing and trompe l'oeil. In addition, they will do exterior painting and all phases of interior repair from Sheetrocking to replacing rotting or damaged wood.

- *"I first saw one of their jobs on a house tour. I fell in love with the way they marbleized the walls. We subsequently had them redo several rooms in our house and a few of them were faux finished. What a difference! I have no difficulty recommending them."*

Janet R. DeBiase Paperhanging, (973)377-0860, UC MC, 10 years in business

A residential wallpaper installer, Janet specializes in English handprints/handscreened paper. She places a great emphasis on the quality of workmanship and attention to detail.

- *"She is excellent with wallpaper. Exceptionally accurate and neat."*

Ray Fein, (908)273-3738, UC MC SC, 30 years in business

Ray Fein is known mainly for wallcovering installation. He will tackle anything from handprints to fabric.

- *"Ray is so detail-oriented. He will do any job to perfection. He has installed so many wallpapers in my house. Some of them were quite difficult and he knew exactly what to do. He works fast and does everything to perfection. As you can tell we have used him over and over."*

Martin Kott Decorating, (732)636-5065, A, 17 years in business

This business deals exclusively with wallpaper. They are known for working with very difficult papers.

- *"He did a wonderful job!"*
- *"I chose a very difficult pattern which was to be hung in a two-story hallway. He had no problem!"*

✍ _____
_____

Libby's, (908)788-4906, MC SC, 7 years in business

Libby Havel considers herself a "color expert." She enjoys assisting her customers in the planning of wall finish and design of the room. After removing wallpaper, she will repair the walls if needed. Her creative stencils reflect her artistic training.

- *"Libby has done stenciling for us in several rooms. She is so creative—we described what we wanted and she created some beautiful stencils. It really added a special touch to the rooms."*
- *"A real talented gal. She has transformed several rooms in my house from ordinary to extraordinary."*

✍ _____
_____
_____

McCullam Unlimited,(908)654-6807, UC, 4 years in business

Interior painting and wallpapering, rather than exterior painting is preferrable for Rob. He will work along with the homeowner as well as with local decorators. He considers himself a perfectionist and claims to look after a client's home as if it was his own.

- *"We had Rob paper our living room. It was a rather difficult job because I had picked out such a busy paper. In addition he had to deal with our nosy dog. He did a beautiful job. Even the dog was his friend."*

✍ _____
_____
_____

Joan Pakenham, (908)232-3901, UC, 9 years in business

Joan incorporates her decorating and artistic background in all her jobs by helping the customer work through the decision-making process to arrive at the look that they want to achieve. Her main focus is on the details whether the work is restoring walls and woodwork or designing and executing decorative finishes. One interesting area of Joan's expertise is custom handpainted designs.

- *". . . very artsy."*
- *"She's loaded with good ideas."*

✍ _____
_____

Robert E. Perry Decorating, (908)522-1987, UC MC SC WC, 18 years in business

Expertise is what makes this wallcovering installer unique. It enables him to handle even the most challenging wallcovering such as handprints, cork, fabrics and all types of vinyls and papers. His eye for color helps in matching paints and wallcoverings.

- *"Bob does the job to perfection. He also cleans up beautifully."*

- *"He painted the entire interior of our home and wallpapered three rooms. No complaints!"*

 _____

John Scott Painting, (908)654-3306, A, 16 years in business

Both wallpaper and painting are John Scott's specialities. As is the nature of the business, he puts a great emphasis on neatness and detail.

- *"Wallpapered our bedroom, bathroom and dining room. He has also done some painting. He moves everything and removes all hardware. I have had painters before who do not do this. I really appreciated that."*
- *"He is meticulous and cleaned up perfectly. He even vacuums."*

 _____

John R. Sweeney, (973)676-5176, A, 30 years in business

Mr. Sweeney considers his business "one-stop shopping." He offers a wide variety of services which include carpentry, restoration, painting, faux marbleizing, and fabric wallcoverings of any type.

- *"He's a perfectionist. He knows how to hand-trim very special and expensive papers."*
- *"He's the kind of person you would want to hire if you had a special job."*

 _____

Wallcoverings by John A. Capra, (973)884-0368, A, 11 years in business

John Capra specializes in wallcoverings including foils, grass cloth, ultrasuede and vinyl. Walls are always fully prepared and he prides himself on neatness.

- *"He's extremely meticulous in his work. A really wonderful perfectionist."*
- *"Very, very neat. I couldn't have cleaned up better myself."*

 _____

WINDOW TREATMENTS

A Delicate Touch, (908)231-0485, UC MC SC MIC, 19 years in business

A Delicate Touch has a large selection of fabric and wallcovering samples to show the customer. They specialize in custom window treatments, wallcoverings, blinds and shades. One nice thing is that they subcontract for the painting or paperhanging needed before custom products are installed, which makes their service unique. It is truly "one-stop shopping at home."

- *"She does wonderful treatments. She has an eye for color and patterns. Some people can't picture certain fabrics together, but she is able to coordinate well."*
- *"She is very serious about pleasing and helping the customer. If they are undecided as to what they want, she has great ideas."*

Creations in Fabric, (973)635-5228, UC MC SC WC, 9 years in business

Janet Agostinelli custom sews for the home. She will make window treatments and coordinate them with bedroom ensembles, pillows, cushions, table rounds, and nursery bedding sets. All work is done in her workshop on the premises.

- *"Working in an Oriental-rug store for many years, I have recommended Creations to many of my customers. She cares about the customer and does a wonderful job in whatever she works on. Everything is always done to perfection. Everyone I know who has used her has been very satisfied."*

Curtain Call Custom Workroom, (908)561-8663, A, 8 years in business

This full-service workroom specializes in unusual treatments and working with specialty fabrics. Curtain Call will design patterns and sew at a couture level. A nice addition is their custom sewing for slipcovers and upholstery.

- *"Does very nice work. Good quality."*
- *"She can do interesting things. She covered tissue boxes for one bathroom and bedroom with matching fabrics to coordinate with my room decor."*

Custom Interiors by Karen, (908)687-0621, A, 9 years in business

This "shop at home" service specializes in custom-made window dressings plus the very latest in privacy shades and blinds. The customer can choose from thousands of fabric samples, many of which are only available through designers. Also custom bed-ensembles can be coordinated with headboards, table skirts and unique decorative pillows.

- *"Karen made silhouettes for our living room, bedroom, kitchen and bathroom. She is a very nice person and knew exactly what I wanted. She delivered and installed them in the time she said she would. She also does upholstery and is scheduled to upholster an antique chair for me."*

• "She installed silhouette shades in three of my bathrooms. Aside from the shades being beautiful, Karen is wonderful to work with. She's very businesslike but creative. She comes prepared with loads of samples."

It's Curtains for You, (973)316-8414, UC MC SC, 10 years in business

Custom window-treatments, soft furnishings, bed ensembles, decorative pillows and more are made by Ellen Gascoigne. She will use the customer's fabric or will help find the appropriate fabric for the job. All measuring, fabrication and installation are done by Ellen.

• "She is fabulous, just wonderful. She does very refined work. She did pillowcases, duvet covers and dust ruffles for bedrooms in my house. She's also professional and does things in a timely fashion."

Passaggio, (908)534-5532, A, 2 years in business

Barbara Valenti feels it's very important to stay on budget when creating window treatments. She will emphasize refurbishing and will attempt to coordinate with existing furnishings if needed. She has access to all New York showrooms for design fabrics and furnishings.

• "Very, very creative. We have used her extensively for window treatments and she has never failed to design and create something that is a real "show stopper.""
• "She's very easy to work with. Has a delightful way of gently guiding the customer to the right decision."

Judith A. Petersen Enterprises, (908)277-3994, UC MC, 25 years in business

Judith is committed to offering premium quality workmanship and service using customer's own materials. Along with specializing in window treatments, she will custom-sew for any other project except for slipcovers and upholstery.

• "The best sewer I know. She does superb work. She's a neat gal."
• "She's done a lot of work for a friend of mine who is a decorator. I know my friend has always been pleased."

Scher Drapery and Design, (800)301-1020, UC MC SC MIC, 30 years in business

All window treatments designed by this company are made and installed by their own craftsmen. They do not use outside installers. Specialities include draperies, top treatments and a full range of shades, vertical woodblinds and almost any decor for windows.

• "They have done all the window treatments in my home. They do exactly what I *want and they do good work. I would—and have—used them over and over again."*

 _____
_____

Vertically Yours, (973)366-4994, A, 13 years in business

As the name implies, all types of window treatments are made by this business They personalize their service to the customer's needs and are flexible enough with their scheduling to work both evenings and weekends.

- *"She's fabulous. She has great taste and is very helpful. She has a good eye for design."*
- *"She installed vertical and miniblinds in my home and we are very pleased with them."*

 _____
_____

Window Scapes, (973)535-5785, UC MC WC, 5 years in business

Window Scapes provides truly custom-order window treatments and any other item that can be fabricated from fabric. All work is done on premises and therefore there are no limitations to what can be done. They unify the customer's likes and needs to create a picture-perfect setting.

- *"I have been very pleased with the window treatments they designed for my living room and dining room. I have received many compliments from friends and relatives and would definitely use them again."*
- *"My sister-in-law has also used them and would recommend them very highly. She was very pleased."*

 _____
_____

Window Treats, (908)232-3849, UC, 5 years in business

Window Treats specializes in providing high-end custom treatments for the home. They will create in addition to window treatments, dust ruffles, duvets, pillow shams, custom bedspreads, table skirts and all types of custom pillows.

- *"Excellent. Reliable. They are nice to work with and timely. Their final results are of an excellent quality."*
- *"I have used them for years and their work always has little special touches. You can give them pictures of very unusual window coverings and they can match it to a 't.' I can go on and on for they do such creative and fabulous work."*
- *"They did my dining room and living room, all-year-round sunporch, master bedroom and guest bedroom and more. Their wonderful personalities make them very easy to work with."*

 _____
_____

WINDOW TREATMENTS

WINDOW WASHERS

ABC Window Cleaning Co., (908)756-2016, UC SC MIC, 36 years in business.
ABC is a small owner-operated window washing service that specializes not only in window cleaning but in glazing and gutter cleaning.
- *"We have used ABC for 10 to 15 years. They are on a schedule for our house four to five times per year and do both inside and outside windows."*
- *"They are very reliable, do a good job and are always on time. We have never had a problem. We do like their service."*

Bound Brook Window Cleaning, (908)356-6555, UC SC, 60 years in business
Jon Ungarten has been in the business for a long time. He provides a window-washing service to residences and businesses.
- *"He is one of my all-time favorite people. I have used him for years and I look forward to his coming two times a year because he is such a delightful person. He also has a real nice crew."*
- *"I would let him work in my house when I am not there for he is very honest and reliable."*
- *"We have used him for eight years. He was recommended by my neighbor. He is honest and friendly and does a superb job! We are always pleased."*

George's Window Cleaning, (908)221-0288, A, 2 years in business
George will clean both windows and gutters. His crew will also do odd jobs for their customers.
- *"He is very good. Very proud of his work. He only works with his family (father and son in business with him). He works with rags only and is very meticulous. My windows really did shine when they were finished."*
- *"Our windows were exceptionally dirty for it was new construction. He was very careful with my window treatments and did a beautiful job."*

Global Window & House Cleaning, (908)709-0491, UC SC, 21 years in business
Global prides themselves on doing a quality job cleaning windows. They are primarily in the residential market and will deal with any type of window.
- *"We have used Tom Lawler for 17 years. He is so accommodating with scheduling. His crew is absolutely fantastic—very considerate of the homeowner. They will even take their shoes off. A wonderful job."*
- *"Having window washers in your home is extremely disruptive all day to the entire home. With Global's guys, they are very careful around window treat-*

ments and considerate of your belongings. They're very pleasant."

✎ _____

_____

Harry's Window Cleaning Co., (732)549-5529, A, 20 years in business
This is a fourth-generation business. The only evidence of their presence is crystal-clear windows. "Everything is done the way the customer wants it done."
- *". . . very good job. Sparkly clean windows and he is extremely careful of my window treatment."*
- *"He does inside-outside and cleans our screens. Will even do little extras such as scrape paint that may be on the windows."*
- *"I have used him for approximately three years and in between I tried some other service which I was not satisfied with and now I am back to Harry's!"*

✎ _____

_____

I Do Windows, Inc., (973)543-7527, MC SC, 14 years in business
I Do Windows uses a special formula that they claim polishes the glass and leaves a bright sheen. This formula will also repel dust, dirt and grime.
- *"We like them very much. We use them one or two times a year and find them to be very nice and very pleasant.*
- *"They are efficient and do a good job including screens. The nice thing is that they can do the whole house in just a couple of hours."*

✎ _____

_____

Menlo Building Maintenance Co. Inc., (732)738-7770, UC SC MIC, 43 years in business
Menlo Building Maintenance is available to the customer 24 hours a day seven days a week! They can schedule your work at times that will cause minimal interference with your "business as usual." Being a complete janitorial company they also offer floor waxing, carpet shampooing, power washing and supplies.
- *". . . very neat, clean job. They are friendly and courteous and did all my lower windows."*

✎ _____

_____

Panestakingly Clean, (908)362-6092, A, 22 years in business
How clean do you want your windows? Panestakingly Clean takes great pride in making windows sparkling clean. They strive to be responsive and return calls promptly.
- *"They are prompt in response to my calls. Very polite and thorough."*
- *"He is so honest that I know I can leave him in my home without worrying."*

✎ _____

_____

Peeping Tom's Window Cleaning, (908)654-9430, UC MIC, 15 years in business

This is a diversified company. Besides window cleaning, which is their main business, they clean gutters, seal decks and driveways and do a little painting.

- *"We have used him over the years for windows and they sparkle when he leaves."*
- *". . . very neat. Really nice guy."*

Rosa Window Cleaning Service Inc., (732)388-5801, UC SC MIC WC, 10 years in business

All work is done by hand by this owner-operated window-washing business. He also offers to his customers gutter cleaning and snowplowing.

- *"He always returns calls and is someone you can count on. He did the job well and fast. He came when he said he would. He also cleaned my gutters. I would highly recommend him."*
- *"I have a three-story house and he was easily able to do it. He was thorough and did a great job. He's a good guy!"*

FOR THE BEACH

We decided to include a small list of businesses that will only service the beach areas. This is primarily for the use of people who own summer homes as it is not terribly comprehensive. A future book is planned for these counties.

APPLIANCE REPAIR

Apple Appliance, (732)223-1286, South Monmouth County, North Ocean County, 12 years in business
Apple will repair anything and everything including all household major appliances. With a great inventory of stock on his truck, he is well-prepared to handle any problem. He tries to supply everyone with same-day service.
- *"Prompt and reliable."*
- *"I am constantly doing wash. My family always teases me that we have a six hour turnaround with clothes. Consequently, when I have a problem with the washer, it's a major problem for me. Apple is there that day working on my washing machine. He's terrific. He's also very quick returning phone calls."*

Neal's Appliance Service, (732)892-5150, Seaside, Ortley Beach, Lavalette, Normandy Beach, Ocean Beach, Point Pleasant, Brielle, Manasquan Mantaloking, Bayhead, Wall Township, Bricktown, Sea Girt, Belmar, 30 years in business
This appliance service tries their best to offer the customer same-day or next-day service except on weekends. They will fix just about anything including: washers, dryers, dishwashers, stoves, and refrigerators.
- *"As a realtor in the Bayhead area, I have had the opportunity to use him on many occasions for rentals. He as always did the job satisfactorily. I have never had a complaint from anyone. When he says he will be there he is."*

CARPENTER

C.W. Applegate Alterations & Repairs, Inc., (732)892-2220, Ocean County, 30 years in business
Alterations, repair work and unusual jobs can all be handled by Applegate. They will also shingle roofs. In addition, they will open and close summer homes, winterize and take care of it in the winter months.
- *"The father and brothers have been in the business for years. They are a well-known name in Bayhead."*
- *"I think very highly of their work as do many others."*

CHIMNEYS

Pete's Chimney Sweep, (732)449-2111, Northern Ocean County, Southern Monmouth County, 20 years in business
Pete's is a full-service chimney company offering the customer a wide variety of services including: waterproofing, relining, chimney caps, new dampers, animal removal, cleaning and home inspections.
- *"Very dependable. We have known him for many years."*
- *"His work is good and he is an honest man. I know when he is finished cleaning my chimney; it is truly clean. We have no hesitation having a fire in the fireplace in the winter."*

GARAGE DOOR INSTALLATION & REPAIR

Mark Sessock Overhead Doors, (732)291-4923, Monmouth County, 13 years in business
Mark Sessock has expertise in the installation and service of overhead garage doors and openers. He will only service residential homeowners.
- *"He uses good quality materials."*
- *"Very efficient guy. He installed a unit about two years ago and we have had no problems."*

GENERAL CONTRACTORS

Van Schoick Builders, Inc., (732)892-3461, Southern Monmouth County, Northern Ocean County, 73 years in business
This is a fourth-generation family-owned company. They will construct a new home and also put on additions. Their love is remodeling older homes and they will use original old materials to a new advantage.
- *"They built my mother's home and it's still standing! She was so pleased with his work. He's very willing to listen and offer great suggestions that we all did not think of."*
- *"This is a reliable, strong family business. I have seen several additions that they have built and added to older homes and they were impressive."*

GLASS REPAIR

Point Pleasant Glass Co., Inc., (732)899-5577, Ocean County, Monmouth County, 37 years in business
This established business will custom-make mirrors, tab enclosures, shower units, and window glass. They will also install storefronts for commercial businesses.
- *". . . made a glass top to fit a custom-made game table. They came and measured and delivered it. No hassles whatsoever and we were definitely pleased with the job."*

HANDYPERSON

Jeff Lee Home Improvements, (732)899-5722, Bayhead Mantoloking, 15 years in business
Here is a true handyman to have in the household directory. At one time or another everyone could use a "Jeff Lee" for window and screen repairs and odd jobs.
- *"He painted the entire exterior of my home. He is a perfectionist."*
- *"He painted the inside of my neighbor's garage and she said that he was so meticulous that it was like he was painting her living room."*

KITCHEN INSTALLATION

Ideal Kitchens, Inc., (732)892-0384, Ocean County, Monmouth County, 28 years in business
Design, manufacturing and installation of all types of cabinetry is the specialty of Ideal Kitchens.
- *"My friend recommended Ideal. She built a beautiful home a few years ago and they put in the kitchen. She was very pleased with the results and thought very highly of the owner."*
- *"Very polite and easy to work with. They always returned phone calls."*

LANDSCAPE DESIGN

Atlantic Plants, (732)920-3536, Ocean County, Monmouth County, 14 years in business
Landscaping and interior plant maintenance is available when you use this family-owned business. Their customized installations bring the home environment back to life.
- *"When we purchased our first beach house, it was in total desperate need of help. Everything was either overgrown or dead. I asked around and Atlantic was recommended several times (I wish I had had this book). So we decided to use them. They really transformed our property and it looked absolutely beautiful. Since then, we went on to another home and continued to use them."*

- *"Their ideas and suggestions are all very good, sometimes so good that it makes it hard to make a decision."*

🖎 _____

_____

_____

Turner Landscape Co., Inc., (732)389-8383, Lower Monmouth County, Upper Ocean County, 19 years in business

What is important to Turner is the desire to provide quality plant material, workmanship and an end product which will make their customers proud. They offer the expertise of design and plant material selection along with a maintenance program.

- *"When I built my home, they presented great landscape plans. They are very good."*
- *"Very, very clever and I am extremely pleased with the results. They are so knowledgeable. They're the tops in the profession."*

🖎 _____

_____

_____

LAWN & TREE MAINTENANCE

R.T. Davies, Inc. Tree Experts, (732)899-0328, Monmouth County, 50 years in business

Davies does pruning, removals, root feeding, planting, consulting and spraying. They pride themselves on their friendly, courteous service.

- *"They are best-known for tree pruning and removal. They have done deep feeding for the roots of my plants. They also do work for my neighbors."*

🖎 _____

_____

_____

C. Macaluso Tree Service & Excavating, Inc., (732)295-3108, Southern Monmouth County, Northern Ocean County, 20 years in business

This is a family-owned-and-operated business. They will perform all phases of tree care for the residential homeowner as well as commercial. Also included are excavating services to include land clearing through final grading.

- *"They were referred to me by my neighbor when we realized one of our trees was dead. As their crew laughed and smiled, they took the tree down. They did a great job and cleaned up their mess."*
- *"Great people to have working for you. They also do pruning."*

🖎 _____

_____

_____

PAINTER

Mantaloking Painting & Carpentry Co., (732)899-3800, Sea Girt to Loveladies, 25 years in business
This company does interior and exterior painting and they will also tackle renovations.
- *"My friend has used him it seems forever. She has never used anyone else for she knows what good work he does and he has never let her down."*
- *"Being very particular about who I have work in my home, they are on the top of my list."*

✍ _____

_____

PLUMBING

Sherman Plumbing & Heating, (732)899-3273, Ocean County, 70 years in business
This business is a wonderful resource for the shore area. It is a third-generation family company emphasizing residential heating and plumbing repair.
- *"Good, fine family business."*
- *"They have worked in my home for years. I trust them implicitly."*

✍ _____

_____

PEST CONTROL

Termite Pest Control, (732)899-9694, Monmouth County, Ocean County, 23 years in business
William Johnson, the owner of Termite Pest Control, does all his own work. He specializes in termites and carpenter ants and will also perform pest-control inspections for the purchase of a new home.
- *"We had a terrible carpenter-ant problem and Mr. Johnson totally solved it."*
- *"He came highly recommended to me and I can highly recommend him to someone else."*

✍ _____

_____

_____

ROOFERS

J.J. Mosteller, (732)295-0182, Monmouth County, Ocean County, 16 years in business
Jeff Mosteller does roofs and a lot more. He is one-stop shopping for home improvements for kitchens, baths, windows, sidewalks, driveway pavings, additions and decks, Sheetrock and painting. All jobs are referrals and he does repeat work for 90% of his customers. His crew does all the work from start to finish and subcontracts when necessary.
- *"He repaired our chimney; did a high quality job. We were exceptionally pleased."*

- *"He had a crew that installed a cedar shake roof for us. This roof has been admired by many people, if you can believe it."*

UPHOLSTERER

Blaine Mori Upholstery, (732)458-1084, Shore Areas, 23 years in business

Blaine will give you an honest evaluation as to whether your piece of furniture is worth upholstering or whether you should buy a new piece. From antiques to contemporary, they offer a personalized service to residential and commercial customers.

- *"Being in the antique business, I needed to find an upholsterer who shares my love of antiques. They fit the bill. They can put the appropriate fabric on these pieces so they look the way they did 1000 years ago."*
- *"Very careful to duplicate an old look."*

WINDOW TREATMENTS

Shore Decorators, (732)892-8818, Ocean County, Monmouth County, 16 years in business

This owner-operated business offers a personal service for custom decorating needs. A workroom is on the premises for slipcovers, upholstery and window treatments.

- *"She does lovely work. When I was in the process of building my home, I was very ill. She worked with me in between all my problems and was able to get everything done in the time I had requested."*
- *"She takes the time to really listen to your ideas. A very honest person."*

WINDOW WASHER

Atlantis Building Maintenance and Point Pleasant Janitorial, (732)458-0700, Ocean County, Monmouth County, 15 years in business

Residential, commercial maintenance along with window cleaning, floor polishing and janitorial service is what Atlantis can do for you. A quote from them: "They will make your business sparkle."

- *"So many of us in our town use their services for window washing. They really try to work with my schedule for I like to be around when any work is done in my home. A trustworthy business."*

ADDITIONAL LISTINGS

The following is a list of businesses that were also highly recommended. They were all contacted. When they responded to our initial phone call, they were asked to return information to us by a specific date. We did not receive the information from them in time to include a description. We have decided to include their names and telephone numbers. Please be advised that although we attempted to verify everything, there may be discrepancies in the business name or telephone number.

ALARM SYSTEMS
Challenger Alarms (973)764-7022
CIA Alarm (908)269-9730
Dan Clark (908)233-2755
A.C. Daughty (973)335-3931
Suburban Alarm (908)233-5252

APPLIANCE REPAIR
L & J Appliance (201)489-9494

CABINETS
Joe Badala (908)232-7665

CARPENTERS
ICD (732)574-9020
Bill Ostenfeld (908)276-7651

CATERERS
Short Hills Caterers (973)379-6950
Steve Soriano (908)722-4411

CHINA & CRYSTAL REPAIR
Brielle Galleries (732)528-8400

**CHRISTMAS DECORATIONS—
OUTSIDE**
Parkers Greenhouses Farm & Garden
Center (908)322-5552

CLOCK REPAIR
Kenilworth Jewelers (908)276-6513

CLOSETS
Closets R Us (908)688-6728

DECORATIVE LIGHTING
Joe Livingstone (908)757-0688

DRIVEWAYS
Mark DiFrancesco (908)668-8434
Nicholas Grace & Sons (908)464-0077
Kristopher Company (908)753-0012

FENCES
Atlantic Fence (732)752-0035
DiPasquale Fence (908)322-5211
Mugan & Sons (908)769-8870

FLOWERS
Bedminster Florist (908)234-2330
Christoffers (908)233-0500
Floral Expressions (908)508-0977

GENERAL CONTRACTORS
Jack Hider (908)526-7176
L.D.S. Renovations (908)467-5862
John Rupp (908)613-8478

GLASS REPAIR
Competitive Glass & Mirror
(908)654-8505

GRANITE FABRICATION
Stonecraft (973)882-7701

GUTTERS
J.P. Bradley (732)238-2727
David Johnson (908)755-4835

HANDYPEOPLE
Mark Russo (908)561-0286

HAULER
Dial a Dump (908)756-3867

HOME THEATER INSTALLATION
Superior Security (732)563-0605

INTERIOR DECORATORS
Mary Ann Tibbles (908)232-1774

KITCHEN & BATH
European Country Kitchens
    (973)781-1554
Leonardis (908)852-4722

LAMP REPAIR
The Lamp Shop (908)273-2795

LANDSCAPE DESIGN
Brandner (908)879-6577
Dubrow (973)992-0598
Brian Feeley (908)647-2130
J & M Plant & Wicker (973)377-4740

LAWN & TREE MAINTENANCE
Four Seasons (908)753-6589
Honor Tree (973)822-0626
Dennis Macaro (908)968-6949
Schmiede (908)322-9109
Woodstack (908)276-5252

MARBLE POLISH
Lincoln Marble (732)381-9098

MASONS
Thomas D'Amore (908)494-3353
John Mastrioni (908)757-9489

MOVERS
Bill Crandall (802)672-3565

MUSICIANS
Ken Michaels (516)829-8310
Steven Scott (908)507-8273
Doug Winters (914)769-0103

PAINTERS
Rob Beal (973)669-8886
Gregg Gullo (908)396-9758
Martin Painters (908)766-9863
New Liberty (973)328-7044
Straight Edge (732)321-0883

PEST CONTROL
Bowco Labs (908)654-3030
Crown Termite (908)322-6288
Humphreys (800)272-1336
Standard (908)889-9484
Terminite (973)353-6938
Western (908)789-0222

PIANO TUNERS
Freehold Music Center (732)462-4730

PLUMBERS
John Burton (908)494-0005
Rich Grant (973)526-1633
Matthew McCarthy (973)228-0128
Ed Mueller (908)356-3719
Robert Rath (973)754-6686

POOL CONSTRUCTION & MAINTENANCE
Gomez Pools (908)756-2895

RAILINGS
Clems (908)968-7200

ROOFERS
Al Caswell (908)968-5183
Hart and Sons (973)761-7676
Mountain View (973)543-5694

SNOWPLOWERS
Romano and Sons (908)789-2293
Tom Wilson (908)322-0513

SPRINKLER INSTALLATION
East Coast Lawn Sprinkler
    (908)968-3045

WALLPAPER
Wallcoverings Ltd. Hegeman
    (908)876-4647

WINDOW CLEANING SERVICES
Skyline Services Inc. (908)699-9181

WINE CELLAR CONSTRUCTION
Leonardis (908)852-4722